recen

Y • Oradea

RUMANIA

Galati
Braila

a

Sad

BUCHAREST
★

Craiova

DE

Giurgiu

Ruse

Lom

Varna

Pleven

SOFIA
★

Skopje

BULGARIA

Hampshire

THE BLUE DANUBE COOKBOOK

Ilona

The
BLUE DANUBE
COOKBOOK

A culinary journey down the Danube,
stopping in Austria, Czechoslovakia,
Hungary, Yugoslavia, Rumania,
and Bulgaria

MARIA KOZSLIK DONOVAN

with illustrations by the author

Doubleday & Company, Inc., Garden City, New York

1967

Library of Congress Catalog Card Number 67–10359

Copyright © 1967 by Maria Kozslik Donovan

Printed in the United States of America

First Edition

CONTENTS

Cakes and Desserts

These recipes were collected in their country of origin by the author and occasionally simplified or adapted for the use of modern cooks.

Recipes for items printed in SMALL CAPITAL letters can be found by consulting the Index.

AUTHOR'S NOTE

A brief explanation is perhaps in order regarding two items you will meet frequently in this book. First, paprika. The best Hungarian paprika comes from the town of Szeged. It is sweet and gives a strong red color to your dishes without too strong a taste. Never use chili pepper when sweet paprika is called for. In case you cannot obtain real Hungarian paprika, you may substitute any sweet paprika. Second, garnishes. You will notice throughout the text that I have used the word "garnish" in referring to decoration and to side dishes. The English word "garnish" is synonymous with the French "*garnir*" and the German "*garnieren*." It means to surround with, decorate, trim. When I say "garnish with rice," the meaning is that the meat is to be surrounded with rice served on the same platter, or served with rice simultaneously offered in a separate dish. "Garnished with lemon, parsley," etc., means "decorated with."

ON THE DANUBE: *An Introduction*

Every major point in Europe is within two hours' flying time from Geneva. Flying becomes more common as prices are slashed in a competitive war by the airlines. Driving a car from Calais to Afghanistan is nothing out of the ordinary any more as long as you carry a Diners' Club card in your luggage. "In" today again are the old-fashioned, mahogany-lined sleeping cars of the Orient Express, where in the twenties Decobra's glamorous spies showed a veiled face and a languid hand behind the curtained window. And one can always rent a gypsy caravan complete with horse and a pack of fortunetelling cards from a hire firm in Connemara, Ireland. But still best is a slow boat down the Danube touching six countries—six small worlds.

The Danube begins its career modestly in the Black Forest. It can be disappointing to stand on the narrow bridge and look down on this Cinderella river, hardly more than an undernourished stream flowing between untidy banks. Especially if this is one's first introduction. But even to the initiated it can come as a shock. The Danube becomes navigable from Passau onward.

I have known and lived near the Danube from the age of eight until I left Hungary after the war. And yet, the first time I drove to the Black Forest from Strasbourg and saw the source, I felt an emotion like that of a grownup confronted with a retarded child. I had to remind myself, by quickly conjuring up in my mind those majestic pictures of the delta, and by remembering the splendid bridges that span the two banks of the twin cities of Budapest, and the steamer trip from Austria right through the Iron Gate and into the Black Sea, that the progress of this retarded child has been one of the great wonders of the world. There are bigger rivers in China, and, compared to the Mississippi, the Río de la Plata, or the St. Lawrence, the Danube is just another of the many rivers on the map. The castles along the Loire or the Rhine outclass such magnificent Danube landmarks as Melk, Visegrad, or Ruschuk. The Île St. Louis on the Seine is historically more famous than Margaret Island, which was a swamp right up to the thirteenth century, when the fair daughter of Hungary's King Bela decided to retire there in monastic seclusion (and which, ironically, six centuries later became a pleasure ground for visiting royalty and oil millionaires from Texas).

Ponte Milvio, on the Tiber, is older than any bridge still standing on the Danube, though the Dacians had fought with the Romans who forded this river long before the Tower of London was built along the Thames.

What is it, then, that makes the Danube unique? It is her charm, the charm of a great actress who has played all kinds of parts in her career. From sophisticated comedies to thundering melodrama she can recite with professional routine the role of an ingénue just as well as that of a tragic queen. From its modest start in the Black Forest the Danube charms, changing face and character each time it traverses a frontier, until it reaches the sea. It begins in the sophisticated West and ends in the mysterious East. Germans, Austrians, Czechs, Hungarians, Yugoslavs, Bulgarians, and Rumanians helped to shape its banks and frequently subdued its wilderness: the Danube has not one national characteristic like the Volga or the Yangtze Kiang, but many facets and many traditions, sometimes conflicting, each adding to its charm. It is the same river, and yet how different is the Danube of Strauss at Vienna from the Duna at Mohács, where in 1526 turbaned Turks fought the Magyars.

Once the Danube flows past the Iron Gate, you enter the Balkans and become aware of the flavors of the East. This territory belonged to the Ottoman Empire for many centuries, and Turkish customs still prevail throughout the countries one traverses as one goes down the Danube. From *Wiener schnitzel* to *kebab* it flows by unperturbed, impervious to the changing languages, customs, politics, man-made frontiers, and even to the Churchillian illusion of a Danube confederation. With great equanimity the river carries steamers, towboats, barges, sailing ships, ferries, and even hydrofoils on its back. It passes under bridges old and new, some bombed and blown up and not reconstructed after the last war. A trip down the Danube is a trip through thousands of years of history as well as a gastronomical exploration.

The countries included in this book have a direct connection with the Danube. They have a close affiliation with each other: until the end of the First World War they belonged, largely, to the Austro-Hungarian Empire. This explains why many of their dishes are basically the same and can be found in different languages in the six countries that border the Danube.

My aim was to select, avoiding as much as possible any repetition, those more typical regional specialities that can be found from the Black Forest to the Black Sea. If there is a predominance of Austrian and Hungarian recipes, it is because the cooking in these so-called mother countries is more eclectic. In the kitchen it is impossible to eradicate a common past. For instance, before the Treaty of Versailles gave the northern part of Hungary to Czechoslovakia, Transylvania to Rumania, and, in the south, Serbo-Croatia to Yugoslavia, the people in these areas lived for centuries, sometimes in peace, sometimes in forced coexistence, with the Magyars. Hungarian cuisine thus owes its variation and also its international reputation to having borrowed freely from these peoples such dishes that appealed to its palate. Such borrowing has been going on for centuries, until it now necessitates patient research to establish which were original Slovak, Serb, Croat, or Rumanian dishes.

And, of course, Austria, who dominated the scene from the heights of bureaucratic Vienna, was equally keen to take over a number of dishes from its loyal subjects, with the result that even today gypsy music is as indispensable in a good Viennese restaurant as in a "Balkan Grill Room," where *kebabs* are grilled side by side with the steaks and chops that will be served Transylvanian style on a wooden platter. Bohemian cooks, who came from Bohemia, part of today's Czechoslovakia, have taught the Austrian housewives the art of making those feather-light dumplings that here are called *Knöderln* and in Prague are known as *knedlíky*. Yoghurt was introduced from Bulgaria, paprika from Hungary, the *givetsch* from Yugoslavia and lamb stew flavored with tarragon from Rumania.

I have lived in or frequently visited each of the six Danube countries, the recipes of which I have collected for this book. Often, before the last war, a difficult choice confronted a Central European who wished to go abroad: should he choose Vienna and its theaters, Salzburg and the festival, or the Tyrol, where fresh mountain air sharpened one's appetite for strudel and chocolate cakes? Or should one go to Yugoslavia, to the Dalmatian coast, where one could sail among the thousands of the Adriatic islands in the summer? In winter for skiing there were the High Tatras of Czechoslovakia; for shooting, the mountains in Rumania, where the hunter could still perhaps come upon a giant bear or add a few antlers to the collection of his trophy room. In spring tradition called for a strict regime and slimming: cures in Bad Gastein, Karlsbad, or Marienbad were advised by the family doctor as a measure against too much goose liver and roast pork that one consumed in winter.

A few years ago in Rome I was seated next to a Dutch diplomat at a dinner, who after the first course turned to me and, to my amazement, addressed me in Hungarian. Now Hungarian is not an indispensable second language on the Continent, as for instance German or French is, and to hear it spoken by a Dutchman was astonishing. But his explanation was simple: he used to go to Hungary on horseback for many consecutive summers. From Austria he rode right down to the south, either following the Danube or riding cross-country into Transylvania. There were many organized holiday trips like those, he told me, which found a large following among sportsmen in Western Europe. I also remember him telling me that his next trip, now that he had reached middle-age, would be by boat . . . a slow boat down the Danube as far as the Black Sea. He asked what I thought of the idea.

I thought his idea excellent. By boat or by car or even on horseback. Through Austria, Czechoslovakia, Hungary, Yugoslavia, Rumania, and Bulgaria. In fact, I still think it such a good program that when I finish this book I would like to be off myself. I would like to start my trip during the cherry season in the Black Forest, take a car to Passau, Bavaria, and there board a steamer. I would like to see once again the unforgettable silhouette of the Abbey of Melk rising above the river; go from Vienna to Budapest and stop for a few days on Margaret Island. Then get on a boat again and cruise down following the great plains and see the majestic gorges around the Iron Gate where once upon a time a train was required to pull the boat over the most difficult part in the course of the river. There the Danube looks almost black because of the reflection of the mountains in its waters. And so down and past the Island of the Roses, the port of Ruschuk and as one nears the delta the reedy marshes where millions of birds nestle and storks, egrets, wild ducks, and sea gulls circle the air above the canals. I should reach the Black Sea in August, where on the beach of Mamaia I could laze and swim by day and, if lucky, have caviar as an hors d'oeuvre at night.

A trip just like I dreamed about ever since I was a child, when I used to press my nose against the windowpane and look down on the embankment, beyond which flowed the Danube, crowned by those glittering, illuminated bridges that resembled the tiaras of old dowagers bobbing up and down at the Vienna Opera Ball.

Genève, March 1966.

MENUS

AN AUSTRIAN DINNER

Chicken Ragout Soup with Liver Dumplings
Fish Gratin "Haus Habsburg"
Crumbed Veal Cutlets
Potato Purée
Cucumber Salad
Cream Strudel
Coffee

* * *

Hühner Ragôut Suppe mit Leberknöderln
Donauschill "Haus Habsburg"
Wiener Schnitzel
Kartoffelpurée
Gurkensalad
Rahmstrudel
Kafé

A CZECHOSLOVAKIAN DINNER

Mushroom Soup
Roast Pork with Dumplings
Stewed Prunes
Linzer Cake

* * *

Houbova Polevka
Veprova Pecene s Knedlíky
Zvestkove-Kompott
Linzertorte

A HUNGARIAN DINNER

Mock Turtle Soup
Whole Filet of Beef
Boiled Rice
Steamed Carrots
Creamed Spinach
Iced Sour Gherkins
Walnut Pancakes

*   *   *

Hamis Teknösbékaleves
Bélszin Egybesütve
Rizs
Sárgarépafözelék
Paraj
Ecetes Uborka
Dióspalacsinta

A HUNGARIAN SUPPER

Goulash Soup
Baked Potato Casserole
Apple Strudel

*   *   *

Gulyás leves
Rakott Burgonya
Almás Rétes

A YUGOSLAVIAN DINNER

Dalmatian Oyster Soup
Turkey with Sauerkraut
Cheese Pie

*   *   *

Ostriga Supa
Podvarak
Gibanica

A RUMANIAN DINNER

Hors d'Oeuvres of Beef Sausages
Consommé
Spring Lamb Cutlets
Potato Purée
Eggplant Salad (Mock Caviar)
Assorted Pastry
Coffee

*   *   *

Mitite
Cotlete Prajite da Miel
Purea de Cartofe
Salata de Vineta
Prájiture
Cafe

A BULGARIAN DINNER

Cold Cucumber Soup
Bulgarian Stew
Plain Yoghurt
Baklava

*   *   *

Tarator
Popska Jachnia
Yoghurt
Baklava

Soups

BONES ARE FOR GOURMETS

Winter came early in 1946. By the beginning of December
the Danube had frozen in patches, making it difficult for the
boats to cross from one bank to the other. Of the seven
bridges that had spanned the river, connecting the old town
of Buda with the business center of Pest, many were blown
up by the retreating armies at the last stages of the war.

Commuters were forced to use every possible means of water transport, from the hastily constructed pontoon bridge to ice hopping, which was the cheapest if not always the safest way. Fishermen gave up fishing and did a lucrative water-taxi business. It was difficult to recognize the once glamorous Budapest, Queen of the Danube, under the layer of snow, ice, bomb-scarred buildings, and broken windowpanes, with the shabby crowds queuing in front of soup kitchens, the general atmosphere of resignation written on their faces.

Food was heavily rationed but almost everything could be obtained at black-market prices from under the counter. Eating became our sole pleasure and to obtain the necessary ingredients for it our constant preoccupation. Farmers in the country would not sell for money; they did not trust the value of the papernotes, with the exception of U.S. dollars. But they would trade eggs, butter, flour, sausages, ham, and poultry for used clothes or golden trinkets. Trains to the country were slow, and one could easily spend twenty-four hours standing in a crowded railway carriage or in the corridor outside when going to some place barely a hundred miles from the capital.

We went with enormous suitcases stuffed with secondhand clothes and fancy bric-a-brac which we hoped would catch the eye of the farmer's wife. I once succeeded in exchanging a pair of mother-of-pearl inlaid opera glasses for a goose.

We played cards, sang, or simply daydreamed about food all through our journey. To speak of food, however, was taboo among friends, much less pardonable even than cheating at cards. Everybody was hungry, everybody knew the dreams of the other, but to say aloud, "*Dobos Torte*" or "*Palacsinta*" was forbidden. If you broke the rule you could easily be black-balled from the exclusive club of food smugglers.

And yet every time we got hold of something rare or tasty we could not resist sharing it with at least a few close friends. Which meant that everybody was always on the go being invited to somebody else's house, and you knew that love was serious when your boy friend was ready to share with you an orange or bring you the roast leg of a goose for which he had exchanged his grandmother's ostrich fan.

Gradually, restaurants began to reopen, and each event was hailed as a major step toward progress and civilization. In these restaurants there were invariably two menus: one that was handed to the ordinary customer who happened to walk in from the street and was unknown to, and therefore not to be trusted by, the proprietor. He could have been a secret agent, a policeman in disguise, and for such a guest potato goulash and dumplings flavored with fried breadcrumbs were all that could be had for a price that was strictly controlled by the government.

But for the regulars who often had to wait patiently until all suspicious-looking customers had left the premises, the owner signaled with a wink from the kitchen door and, pressing his forefinger to his lips, would disappear to come back, when all was clear, with a succulent plate of black-market roast or a piece of goose liver worth its weight in gold. Thus the word passed around in whispers that the best *Wiener schnitzel* could each day be had in a restaurant near the Opera House, or that a certain place had contacts with the Russian Army and had therefore an unlimited supply of game. (Shooting, the favorite pastime of Hungarians, was forbidden, with exceptions made only for high government officials or reliable Party members. Shotguns had to be handed in, and since there were no private cars circulating in the countryside, there was little chance of "running over" a hare on the road.)

Since it was a bitterly cold winter, that year of 1946, everybody was even hungrier than usual. Espresso-type coffee shops, always the favorites with Hungarians, sprang up like mushrooms on every street corner. There you could always rely on an excellent cup of coffee, and if it happened to be your regular coffeehouse, a dash of whipped cream was quickly slapped over your coffee or you could ask it to be laced with brandy or rum. People seemed to be living their whole lives in these places: they went to the coffeehouse not just to meet friends but also to do business there, clinch a deal, or listen to the latest and hottest news about the political situation. As quickly as the coffee shops were opened they were also just as often closed down by the police, with the owner disappearing for months, sometimes forever.

The coffee shop with the most romantic atmosphere was the one opened by a princess in her own centuries-old town house near the bombed-out royal castle. Here too, if you were a friend or a regular, you could rely on being served not just with coffee but with excellent dishes as well, prepared by the old chef of the proprietress, who used to cook for visiting kings and was famous for his parfait ices and *crêpes Suzette*. Bearded and bewhiskered ancestors and bejeweled ladies in court dress glared down from the walls on the "guests" and seemed to be shaking their heads with disapproval whenever the princess handed the bill to a customer who, overawed and somewhat ill at ease, never failed to leave an even larger tip than he would have done elsewhere.

My favorite place, however, had none of the noble atmosphere of this princely restaurant-cum-coffee shop. It was a simple pub, only a block removed from the Houses of Parliament, with its neo-Gothic spires, and a stone's throw from the Danube, from where an icy wind whistled through the street as one turned the corner. Only one room with some eight or ten small tables and in the background the barrels—most of them empty—where the proprietor kept his wines before the war. He came from the district of Lake Balaton, famous for wines like the *Badacsonyi Kéknyelü*, the *Szürkebarát*, and the *Hárslevelü*. His eating house had stood for forty years on the same place and he had inherited it from his father.

For forty years also, I suppose, the menu had not changed. Or better still, there had never been a menu. There was no need for it, since here one could get only one dish. But it was a complete meal in itself. It was boiled beef with vegetables: first the bones served, then the soup, and lastly the meat surrounded with the boiled vegetables. There was always a separate plate of freshly grated horseradish to make your eyes smart.

The customers were almost exclusively men. It is known that the world is divided into two distinct categories: soup eaters and non-soup eaters. Men are soup eaters. Children as a rule hate soup. Unmarried women following a busy career cannot be bothered with the time to make it. Only housewives with a streak of old-fashioned simplicity to their character appreciate a good soup, and they know that nothing from a package or out of a can can substitute for what the French call *la grande marmite*. Men like to sit down to a table (in some countries they even tuck their serviettes into their collar) and look forward to beginning the meal with a steaming hot plate of soup.

Here in this pub there was a ceremony that went with the serving of the *specialité de la maison*. First, the owner approached the guest with two liqueur glasses filled with a colorless liquid. He offered one to the customer, raised his glass, and drank a toast with him. It was Hungarian apricot brandy (*Barackpálinka*) a strong, exquisite apéritif. With this ritual over, the waiter brought from the kitchen a plate of bones and freshly toasted bread. One end of each bone was neatly wrapped in tissue paper to make it easy to pick up, and the moment that the guest shook the marrow from the bone and began spreading it thickly over his toast was the most important part of the meal.

Marrowbones on toast are a gourmet's delicacy. And so is boiled beef, and so is the soup, a clear bouillon, golden yellow in color, with that narrow rim of fat like a frame encircling the plate. In Vienna, birthplace of the cult of boiled beef, those who appreciate this dish would walk miles to their favorite restaurant, where they know that the *Tafelspitze* or *Beinfleisch* was of the best quality.

Boiled beef with its soup was a strong tradition in the Austro-Hungarian monarchy. It was known in all the Danube countries, from Czechoslovakia to Rumania. And I suppose what really contributed to the disintegration of the monarchy, and with it the custom of a leisurely life, was not just the political differences among its polyglot countries, but also the appearance on the market of the bouillon cube. You may prepare an instant hot soup with a cube, but someone has yet to invent the instant-frozen-prepackaged marrowbone.

SOUPS

Beef Broth

(RINDFLEISCH SUPPE ODER KONSOMME)

Austria

2½ pounds boiling beef (shin or brisket end of flap)	1 lump sugar
	1 large red onion
2 pounds beef bones (marrowbones)	3 carrots, sliced lengthwise
2½ quarts water	2 parsnips, sliced
Salt	1 stick celery
2 bay leaves	½ root celery (if obtainable)
8 peppercorns	

Wash meat and bones, then place in a deep saucepan and cover with cold water. Add salt, bring to boil, and skim froth off carefully. Let cook, very slowly, for 1 hour. Now add the bay leaves, peppercorns, sugar, and red onion (in the whole, with its outer skin left on), the carrots, parsnips, and celery and continue boiling for another hour or two.

Line a strainer with a clean cloth and pass soup through it, skimming it this way of all fat. (Another way to clarify soup is to add a beaten egg white to it, which brings all grease and impurities to the top. Or, easiest still, prepare the soup a day before, put in the refrigerator, and next day lift off the fat.) (Serves 8.)

Dalmatian Oyster Soup

(OSTRIGA SUPA)

Yugoslavia

This soup, though ideal for those who live or vacation on the coast, can still be prepared in a modern kitchen in town, provided always that the housewife has an access to a good fish dealer who can supply her with the bones, heads, small fish that are essential to make the stock. If fresh oysters are unobtainable or expensive, you may use bottled oysters from the supermarket.

4 tablespoons oil	5 peppercorns
2 cloves garlic	1 bay leaf
2 teaspoons parsley	2 slices toast
1–2 pounds fishbones, heads, small fish	½ cup dry white wine
2 quarts water	Juice of ½ lemon
Salt	1–2 dozen oysters

In a large saucepan heat oil and fry the chopped garlic and parsley for a few minutes. Add the fishbones, heads, small fish and cover with cold water. Season with salt, peppercorns, and bay leaf. Bring to boil without a lid and let cook rapidly for 20 minutes. Strain very carefully and discard bones and small fish, obtaining thus a clear stock.

Cut toast into long strips. Place these in the soup dishes. Reheat the stock with the white wine added. Remove from the fire, add the lemon juice and oysters. Pour this hot soup over the toasted bread strips and serve.

(Serves 4–6.)

Fresh Tomato Soup with Semolina Dumplings

(PARADAJZ CORBA SA GRIZ KNEDLAMA)

Yugoslavia

For the soup:

2 *pounds fresh tomatoes*   3 *tablespoons oil or lard*
  (*or a 2-pound 3-ounce can*   2–3 *cloves garlic*
  peeled tomatoes)   2 *teaspoons chopped*
Salt   *parsley*
Freshly *ground black*   1 *tablespoon plain flour*
  pepper to taste   1 *teaspoon sugar*
1–2 *teaspoons hot chili*
  pepper

For the semolina dumplings:

2 *tablespoons butter*   ¾ *cup sifted flour*
2 *eggs, separated*   Salt
4 *tablespoons semolina*

Quarter and cook fresh tomatoes in a pint of water (or use canned tomatoes) seasoned with salt and peppers. After about a half hour strain through a fine wire sieve but retain liquid.

Heat oil in a separate saucepan and fry lightly the garlic and chopped parsley. Blend in flour, fry till golden in color, then dilute with strained tomato liquid, stirring all the time to avoid lumps in the flour. Mix in pulp of tomatoes, add sugar, and bring soup to boil without a lid. Keep boiling slowly while you prepare dumplings as follows:

Cream butter with yolks of egg, add semolina, flour and salt. Beat separately until stiff the whites of egg and fold in carefully

with the semolina mixture. With the help of a spoon cut dumplings from this batter and drop into boiling soup. Cook for
10 to 15 minutes until all dumplings have risen to the surface.
(*Serves 6.*)

Tripe Soup

(DRSTKOVA POLEVKA)

Czechoslovakia

1 *pound tripe*	1 *bay leaf*
2 *quarts water*	2–3 *large sprigs parsley*
4 *onions, sliced*	1 *tablespoon corn flour or*
2 *carrots, diced*	*potato flour*
Salt	
Freshly ground black	
pepper	

Soak tripe for several hours in cold water. Cut into small
squares. In a large saucepan (or ovenproof casserole with a
lid) place the onion, carrot, and tripe and cover with cold
water. Season with salt and pepper, bay leaf, and parsley.

Cover saucepan or casserole with its lid, bring to boil on top
of the stove. Now transfer into a very low (200°) oven, where
it should barely simmer for 4 hours.

Thicken at last with corn flour or potato flour and serve hot.
(*Serves 6.*)

Caraway-seed Soup

(KMINOVA POLEVKA)

Czechoslovakia

2 tablespoons butter	1¾ quarts water
2 tablespoons flour	Salt
1 teaspoon Hungarian	Freshly ground black
sweet red paprika	pepper
2 tablespoons caraway	Diced bread
seeds	Butter

In a saucepan heat the butter and lightly fry the flour. When
golden, sprinkle with paprika and caraway seeds. Carefully

dilute, while stirring all the time, with enough cold water to make 4 to 6 plates of soup. Season with salt and pepper.

Bring soup to boil, uncovered. Reduce heat immediately and let simmer gently for 20 minutes. Strain through a very fine wire sieve to eliminate caraway seeds. Fry bread in a little butter or cooking fat and serve separately (like snippets) with the soup. (*Serves 4.*)

Mushroom Soup

(HOUBOVA POLEVKA)

Czechoslovakia

The forests of Czechoslovakia are famous for their mushrooms. So abundant do they grow in season that a lot of them are dried and preserved to keep the housewife in mushrooms all year round.

To preserve mushrooms, you have to avoid washing them. Slice finely the cap and part of the stalk, and spread on a large tray where mushrooms must dry for several days, preferably outside in the open. When mushrooms are dry, keep them in bags made of butter muslin in a dry and cool place.

½ pound fresh mushrooms (or 1 ounce dried mushrooms)	2 quarts water Salt
Approximately 1 pound veal bones	2 tablespoons butter 1 tablespoon chopped parsley
1 carrot	2 tablespoons flour
1 small onion	Freshly ground black pepper
1 parsnip or turnip	

Wash well but do not peel the fresh mushrooms. Slice or roughly chop. (If using dried mushrooms, soak them previously in warm water for at least an hour. Discard water and chop mushrooms in equal pieces.) Make a stock from the veal bones, carrot, onion, parsnip or turnip by boiling them in salted water. After about one hour and a half, discard bones but retain vegetables, which should be puréed and added to the soup.

In a separate saucepan heat butter, add the chopped mushrooms and parsley. Cover with lid and let steam without adding any water, for 10 minutes. Take lid off, blend mushrooms with flour, stirring for a few minutes. Pour the stock over them carefully, season with pepper. Let it boil, uncovered, for some 15 minutes more. Serve hot.
(*Serves 6.*)

Potato Soup

(BRAMBOROVA POLEVKA)

Czechoslovakia

4 large potatoes	½ cup milk
2 quarts salted water	1 egg yolk
1½ tablespoons butter	Salt and pepper
1 carrot, finely sliced	Fried, diced bread
1 tablespoon flour	(optional)
1 tablespoon chopped parsley	

Peel, dice, and boil the potatoes in salted water. When cooked, strain potatoes through a wire sieve and retain the liquid. Meanwhile in a separate saucepan heat the butter and add the carrot. Cover with lid and steam (without adding any liquid) for 15–20 minutes. Take off lid, blend carrot with flour, sprinkle with parsley. Fry the flour for a few minutes, then dilute with milk and cook for another few minutes. Add the potatoes and dilute the mixture with the potato water to obtain the consistency

of a creamy, thick soup. Heat a soup dish, pour in soup, and
lastly add the beaten egg yolk. You may offer separately fried
and diced bread.
(*Serves 6.*)

Goulash Soup

(GULYAS LEVES)

Hungary

Very few people know that the secret of a real Hungarian
goulash lies in the amount of onions. Contrary to popular
belief, it is not the onions that make a goulash. Nothing hor-
rifies a Hungarian cook more than to read recipes supposedly
for goulash where more than one medium-sized onion is used
to the quantity of a pound of meat.

The consistency of a real goulash should be just a shade
thinner and more liquid than a correctly made Italian *minestrone.* Another important factor is the meat. Shin beef (the
muscular, gelatinous part of the lower leg of the beef) should
be asked for from the butcher, in order to cook a perfect
goulash.

1 *pound shin beef, cut into cubes*	2 *teaspoons (or more) Hungarian sweet red paprika*
1 *medium-sized red onion*	
3–4 *medium-sized potatoes*	Salt
2 *tablespoons bacon fat or lard*	2 *quarts water*

Cut meat into small cubes and finely chop the onion. Peel and
quarter the potatoes. In a large saucepan melt the fat or lard
and fry onion until golden in color. Blend in the paprika and
add the meat immediately. Fry the meat thoroughly, stirring

all the time. Add salt. Reduce heat, cover with lid, and cook without adding more than an occasional spoonful of water. At the same time, in a separate saucepan cook potatoes in salted water. When potatoes are cooked, add their cooking liquid to the meat, lastly add the cooked potatoes. Cooking time required for this dish is approximately one and a half hours for the meat and 20 minutes for the potatoes.
(*Serves 8.*)

Mock Turtle Soup

(HAMIS TEKNOSBEKA LEVES)
Hungary

Real turtle soup is one of the greatly appreciated delicacies among gourmets. A live turtle and its fresh blood are used for it, and the procedure requires the skill of a professional cook. In Hungary we like this mock turtle soup, which is made with the meat of a calf's head and, when served, the little meat balls look deceptively like real turtle meat.

1 calf's head	Cayenne pepper
1 pound calf's bones (or 1–2 calf's knuckles)	1–2 egg yolks
10 cups water or, preferably, canned bouillon	3 tablespoons butter
	4 tablespoons flour
	½ glass dry red wine
Salt	1 liqueur glass Madeira wine or brandy

Cook calf's head and bones (or knuckles) in salted water, or, for an even more satisfactory result, in canned bouillon. When meat is tender, take carefully off the bone. Discard bones. Strain the cooking liquid through a sieve. Retain liquid. Mince the cooked meat, season with salt, cayenne pepper, and mix with the yolk or yolks of egg. Shape small balls with your hands (the size of small marbles).

Heat the butter in a separate saucepan. Fry the flour in butter for a few minutes, then dilute with the soup liquid. Correct seasoning, adding, if necessary a little cayenne pepper. Add also the glass of red wine and let the soup simmer, without a lid, for a quarter of an hour.

Now add the meat balls and boil for 5 minutes. Lastly, just before serving, pour on the Madeira wine or brandy. (*Serves* 8.)

Sauerkraut Soup

(KAPOSZTALEVES)

Hungary

This soup is a tradition in Hungary. They used to serve it in the small hours of the morning after a ball. It is supposed to clear the heads of revelers and cure hangovers.

½ *pound fresh sauerkraut* (*or 1 can*)	1 *tablespoon flour*
	Salt
8 *cups cold water*	6–9 *peppercorns*
2 *slices bacon, diced*	½ *pound frankfurters* (*or*
1 *onion, finely chopped*	*dried paprika* (*Polish*)
2 *teaspoons Hungarian*	*sausage*)
sweet red paprika	4 *tablespoons sour cream*
2 *teaspoons caraway seed*	

Set the sauerkraut to boil in a saucepan in the water. (If canned and cooked sauerkraut is used, you need only to heat it to boiling point, with the water added.) Cook fresh sauerkraut for three-quarters of an hour.

In a separate saucepan fry the bacon and in the fat fry the onion. Sprinkle with the paprika and add caraway seed. Blend flour with the onions and, after frying it a few minutes, dilute with liquid in which you cooked the sauerkraut. Correct seasoning with the necessary salt, adding also the peppercorns.

Put into saucepan the cooked sauerkraut and the frankfurters, cut up, or dried sausage, cut up. Bring all ingredients to a boil, stir and mix well, and let cook, without a lid, for 15 minutes.

Just before serving, add, off the fire, the sour cream. (*Serves 8–10.*)

Ham-bone Soup

(KASZASLE)

Hungary

This soup is the ideal answer to the problem of what to do when one comes to the end of the Christmas or Easter ham. But, naturally, one can make it on other occasions as well, obtaining a knuckle of ham for it. This soup should have a distinctly tart flavor.

½ pound stewing pork (or smoked pork)	*4 cloves garlic*
	4 tablespoons flour
Knuckle of ham (already cooked)	*½ cup sour cream*
	1 egg
2½ quarts water	*3–4 tablespoons white wine vinegar*
Salt	

Cut stewing pork into small cubes and dice the ham you have cut off the knuckle. In a saucepan put cold water to cover pork and diced ham. Add seasoning (careful with salt!), the whole cloves of garlic, cover with lid, and let simmer until pork is tender.

In a mixing bowl blend flour with sour cream and also the egg. Thicken soup, off the fire, with the mixture of sour cream and egg. Keep stirring with a wooden spoon, and lastly, just before serving, add vinegar. (*Serves 8.*)

Lamb Soup

(SOFIA CORBA)
Bulgaria

This is a typical Bulgarian soup, a *čorba* (pronounced *tshorba*) which is half soup, half stew. You shall encounter the *čorba* also in Yugoslav cooking, and even in the southern parts of Hungary. The Rumanian *čorba* is called generally a *bors* (from the Russian *borscht*).

1 *pound stewing lamb*	2 *teaspoons chopped fresh*
4 *onions*	*mint*
2 *carrots*	10 *cups lukewarm water*
1 *turnip*	½ *cup uncooked rice*
4 *tablespoons vegetable oil*	½ *cup plain yoghurt*
Salt	
Freshly ground black	
pepper	

Ask your butcher to give you stewing lamb and cut meat into small cubes. Slice onions finely, dice vegetables. Fry meat in oil in a large skillet or casserole till all of it changes color (about 3–5 minutes). Add onion, vegetables, salt, pepper, and mint. Cover with lid, reduce heat, and let simmer for three-quarters of an hour. If necessary, moisten now and then with a few tablespoonfuls of cold water.

Wash and dry the rice, add to meat, stir well. Pour on lukewarm water, bring to boil, then quickly reduce heat and let gently simmer until rice is cooked—about 12 minutes, no more.

Just before serving, blend in the yoghurt, but take care not to let soup boil with it. (*Serves 8.*)

Iced Cucumber Soup

(TARATOR)

Bulgaria

This is the most delicious of all cold summer soups. It is of Turkish origin. Those who are tired of the *gazpacho* that, together with the obligatory Costa Brava holiday, has lost its novelty, should try serving *tarator* in summer before a barbecue dinner.

3–4 large fresh green cucumbers	2–3 cloves of garlic, crushed
Salt	4 ounces coarsely chopped walnuts
4 cups plain yoghurt	
4 cups water	2–3 tablespoons olive oil

Peel cucumbers and finely chop. Sprinkle with salt, place in a china bowl, cover with a lid, and keep in the refrigerator for at least one hour.

Dilute the plain yoghurt with the cold water. Add the garlic and walnuts.

Prepare a deep china or glass bowl by rubbing sides with additional garlic. Put in the chilled cucumber and mix with the garlic- and walnut-flavored yoghurt and water. Blend very well with the olive oil and chill thoroughly. Serve directly from the refrigerator.
(*Serves 4–6.*)

Chicken Ragout Soup with Liver Dumplings

(HUHNER RAGOUT SUPPE MIT
LEBERKNODERLN)

Austria

The Soup:

The giblets, feet, neck, wings of a chicken	4 carrots, diced
10 cups water	2 stalks celery, chopped
1 small veal knuckle bone	1 red onion, chopped
Salt	1–2 parsnips, diced
8 peppercorns	2 tablespoons chopped parsley
2 tablespoons butter	2 tablespoons flour

Clean and prepare chicken giblets, feet, neck, and wings. In a saucepan set them in *cold* water with the veal bone, salt and peppercorns. Allow to simmer, covered, for 1½ to 2 hours. Meanwhile in a separate saucepan heat the butter and in it cook the vegetables, covered, in their own steam. Take off lid, dust vegetables and parsley with flour, and carefully, while stirring with a wooden spoon, dilute with the chicken stock, strained. Discard feet, but put back rest of giblets and wings and neck to the soup.

The Liver Dumplings:

2 slices white bread,
  soaked in milk
¼ pound liver (chicken
  or calf's)
½ red onion, minced
1 tablespoon butter

1 teaspoon chopped
  parsley
Salt and pepper to taste
1 egg
2 tablespoons breadcrumbs

Soak bread in a little milk, squeeze dry. Put bread and liver through a grinder. Fry the onion in butter till golden and also the parsley. Put liver-bread mixture in a mixing bowl, add the fried onion and parsley and seasoning. Mix with egg and sift in breadcrumbs.

Dust your hands with flour and shape small balls, the size of a large marble, with the mixture. Bring the soup to fast boil, drop in dumplings one by one, and cook until they rise to the surface.
(*Serves 8.*)

Leek Soup with Potatoes

(PORREESUPPE MIT KARTOFFELN)

Austria

4 leeks (the white parts
  only)
2 tablespoons butter
4 medium-sized potatoes,
  thinly sliced
Salt and pepper

1 pint water or canned
  bouillon
2 tablespoons chopped
  parsley
Diced bread, fried in
  butter

Finely slice the white part of the leeks. Heat the butter in a saucepan, add leeks, and cook for 15 minutes in their own steam. Add potatoes, salt and pepper, and pour the water or bouillon, heated to boiling point into the saucepan. Reduce heat and cook, covered, for 20 more minutes, or until potatoes become almost a purée. Serve with freshly chopped parsley sprinkled on top, and offer separately diced bread fried crisply in butter.
(*Serves 6.*)

Haricot Bean Soup (Hot)

(BOHNEN SUPPE)

Austria

1 cup white haricot beans	1½ tablespoons cooking fat
2 quarts water	1 teaspoon chopped
3 slices bacon, diced	parsley
Salt	2 tablespoons flour
2 bay leaves	4 frankfurters, sliced
Freshly ground black	Vinegar to taste (optional)
pepper	Diced bread

Soak beans overnight, drain, and set to boil in cold water, together with the bacon, salt, bay leaves, pepper. Cook until beans are soft, drain them through a wire sieve, and keep all the liquid. Prepare a light thickening by heating the fat in a saucepan and adding the chopped parsley and the flour. Fry flour until golden in color, dilute with the liquid off the bean soup, and let it boil for 15 minutes. Add the strained beans and the frankfurters and reheat thoroughly. You may flavor the soup with a few drops of wine vinegar. Serve soup hot, with fried bread offered separately.
(*Serves 6.*)

Bean Soup (Cold)

(SUPA DE FASOLE)

Rumania

This very thick soup, almost like a vegetable purée, is a traditional dish during Lent in the Orthodox part of Rumania. It is
eaten cold and differs quite substantially from the ordinary
bean soup, since it has a distinct garlic flavor.

1 cup small white haricot beans	Freshly ground black pepper
4 carrots	3 tablespoons salad oil
Salt (preferably coarse-grained cooking salt)	4 cloves garlic, crushed

Soak beans overnight in cold water. Drain, put into a saucepan with sufficient lukewarm water to cover. Dice carrots and
add to the beans. Season with salt. Bring to boil, cover, and
reduce heat to a bare simmer. By adding frequently a little
more cold water to the beans, you let them cook for exactly
4 hours.

The purée of beans and carrots that results from the cooking
is now put into an earthenware dish and allowed to cool
thoroughly. Just before serving it (cold), prepare it rather like
a salad, by seasoning the beans with plenty of freshly ground
black pepper and dressing it with salad oil (in Rumania walnut
oil for Lent!). It is important that the beans should be touched
only with a wooden spoon and never with metal.

Lastly, sprinkle the freshly crushed or chopped garlic on top.
(Serves 6.)

Sheep's-Head Soup

(BORS DE MIEL)

Rumania

This soup is a great Easter Sunday specialty in Rumania. The head of a sheep, preferably that of a young spring lamb, is served to each person on a plate, with a delicate consommé poured over it. Lamb is the symbol of Easter, and in Rumania the resurrection ceremony begins at midnight on Saturday, with the worshipers each holding long, thin tapers that will be lit from the Easter candle held by the priest.

4 heads of spring lamb	4 egg yolks
Salt	1 cup sour cream
6 white onions	Ground white pepper
3 small carrots, diced	
1 celery stalk and leaves, diced	

Pour boiling water over the lamb's heads, clean them thoroughly, but do not remove either the eyes or the tongue. Place in a very large saucepan with enough lukewarm water to cover. Add salt, the whole onions, carrots, and celery. Bring to boil, reduce heat and let simmer under cover for 2 hours.

In a mixing bowl blend the egg yolks (allowing always 1 yolk per person) with the sour cream and season with white pepper. Beat hard with a wire whisk until well blended and frothy. Now strain the hot soup into this egg and cream mixture, stirring all the time to avoid curdling. Place 1 head into each plate and pour the soup over it.

(Serves 4.)

Fish, Poultry, and Game

A BEAR HUNT WITH CAVIAR

Travel brochures used to call Bucharest the little Paris of
the East. The Rumanians did not object: they were Francophile
in their sympathy, and French was the second language spoken
in society as well as in the elegant shops that tried to re-create
an atmosphere of the Faubourg St. Honoré. The Rumanians
are a gay people who before the war liked to stroll in the

streets twice a day—before lunch and late in the afternoon—admiring the beautiful girls and the elegant women with the same open effusiveness that one finds in Latin countries. Night life was flourishing and so were the café houses and the little intimate bars. In summertime, when Bucharest becomes oppressively hot, open-air restaurants used to attract large crowds, who liked to wine and dine, listening to the gypsy orchestras till the small hours of the morning.

In the best hotel, called the Athenée Palace, East met West, and one could watch with endless fascination the life of this strange city. Shortly after the war, when Rumania, like the rest of Central and Eastern Europe, was in the throes of inflation, I spent almost one year living at the Athenée Palace. I doubt that there exists a language in this world of which you could not pick out a few strands while sitting in the bar or pretending to read the daily papers in the Edwardian setting of the lounge. It was here that four of us, a French couple, an American colonel with the Allied Control Commission, and myself met one morning to discuss plans for a bear hunt in the Carpathians.

The colonel had hunted for bear in Alaska and for tigers in Burma. I was brought up on game in Hungary and used to go after hare, pheasant, and wild duck, but bears I had seen only in the circus. The French couple, being skeptical, suggested the gambling casino in the mountain resort of Sinaia. We shall go through Sinaia, the colonel reassured them, but first we must discuss the program over a glass of champagne and caviar.

Next door to the Athenée Palace, the Ikra Bar was one of the unique features of this "little Paris." In fact, the French couple maintained that nothing like that ever existed in Montmartre or even on the Champs Elysées, and if one wished to eat caviar by the spoonful at the Tour d'Argent . . . O là là!

You entered the Ikra Bar through a small, unpretentious door and found yourself in a shop. The goods displayed under a glass counter were nothing but cans, small and large, of caviar. Forty-four varieties, as the white-coated owner explained to us in a matter-of-fact voice. You pick the sort you like best and proceed next door. The waiter will see to the rest.

Through an open arch you came into the "bar." A dozen tables, no more, and each numbered with a large number in black. No decorations, no atmosphere. In fact, one wall was entirely given over to what looked like a giant refrigerator, with twelve doors, bearing the same numbers as the tables. We sat down and waited. After a few minutes the waiter came in, bringing the cans we had selected outside. He opened the door of the refrigerator that corresponded with our table number, and put the cans inside. Then he closed it airtight and, stepping to our table, inquired which brand of champagne we preferred. Having taken our order for Veuve Cliquot, he disappeared, to return with two bottles, which he similarly enclosed in the refrigerated wall safe.

Nobody seemed to be in a hurry: the pace was leisurely and the hours elastic in Bucharest. We sat, going into the details of the hunt, which was to take place in two days' time, and a good half hour went by before we saw our waiter again. This time he brought the champagne bucket and ice and a silver dish with whipped cream. Another dish with chopped raw onions and a third, with lemon slices, followed. On the table before us we each had a spoon, a small plate, and a champagne glass. Nothing could have been more simple and less exciting.

And then the caviar arrived. Directly from the refrigerator the cans were produced, opened, and placed one before each of us. The waiter filled the glasses and, stepping back, watched anxiously as the first spoon disappeared inside the grayish-black, glutinous mass, the finest Black Sea caviar, which was flown to Bucharest each day. Is it chilled enough? the waiter asked. Is the cream fresh, do you wish for some black bread, is everything all right?

Everything was, but, never again, I am sure, could any one of us muster up as much enthusiasm over a thin cracker spread with a few grains of caviar as it gets offered at cocktails in the West. The precious stuff, the pearl of the sea! Every ten minutes or so, as he refilled our glasses, our waiter took the cans away and popped them back inside the refrigerator for a little more chilling. This way we hardly realized that some two hours later we each had consumed a pound of caviar before going on to lunch from the Ikra Bar.

Outside, the early October sun was shining and one could already detect a nip in the air. The best time of the year, the colonel said, to go for the bear in the Carpathians. The mountain berries have ripened, the bears come down from their hiding places, and, like gluttonous children, gorge themselves on the black fruit. They trample through the scrubby undergrowth and, so absorbed are they in their gourmandizing, that the hunter can approach within a few feet of them.

Two days and some hundreds of kilometers later, we did indeed see our first bear. The jeep came to halt on the market square of a fair-sized town in what used to be Transylvania before the First World War.

The bear stood on his hind legs and he had a ring through his nose. To the sound of a drum he was slowly, sadly lifting a clumsy foot a few inches from the ground. He clapped his hands, too. Children and people from the country who came to the market stood around him and his sheepskin-clad owner. They stared and laughed at the bear. Then a small child walked up to him fearlessly and offered the captive animal a basket. The bear tried to get his paw inside, but it was too big. So the child spilled the contents on the ground and the bear, forgetting his chain, sat down with a thud and fell on the berries with a voracious appetite. His owner was still beating on the drum but the bear did not hear it: he was eating happily, his face smeared all over with the dark red fruit just as if he were back in the mountains, free to roam among the berry bushes once again.

FISH

Fish Gratin "Haus Habsburg"

(DONAUSCHILL "HAUS HABSBURG")

Austria

This recipe is one of the specialties of the famous Restaurant Zur Spanische Hofreitschule in Vienna. The Spanish riding school with its magnificent white stallions who dance and prance to music are the pride of the Viennese.

The fish used for this dish is fillet of *Donauschill*—the finest Danube fish. A very good result, however, is obtained, by using whiting fillets, fresh or frozen, if one is not able to get the *Donauschill*. I have also simplified the recipe for household use.

4 tablespoons butter	½ cup shelled shrimp,
A little plain flour	fresh or frozen
Milk	½ cup canned button
Salt	mushrooms
White pepper	4 thin slices smoked ham
8 fillets whiting, sole, or	Grated Parmesan cheese
flounder (fresh or frozen)	

Prepare a white sauce with 2 tablespoons butter and a little flour and milk—enough to make 2 cups. Season carefully with salt and white pepper. Wash the fish fillets, dry, and dust with flour. Heat 2 tablespoons of butter in a frying pan and fry fillets on both sides till light golden. Remove and place in a well-greased ovenproof dish. In the same frying pan heat the shrimp and the mushrooms.

Cut into 2 pieces each thin slice of ham and place on top of the fish fillets. Surround with the shrimp and mushrooms and pour the white sauce over it all. Sprinkle generously with grated Parmesan cheese and brown under the broiler. (*Serves 4.*)

Baked Carp (*or any whole fish*)

(PLACHIA DE CRAP)

Rumania

Though in Rumania, where rivers are plentiful, this dish is always made with carp, you can apply the same method to any large, whole fish, even sea fish.

1 carp or other fish	*2 ripe, fresh tomatoes,*
weighing about 3 pounds	*sliced*
½ cup white wine vinegar	*12–18 black olives*
½ cup cold water	*1 bay leaf*
Salt	*Sprig of thyme*
2 medium-sized onions,	*8 black peppercorns*
sliced	

Wash, scale, and clean out insides of fish but leave on head, fins, and tail. Place in an earthenware dish, pour over it the vinegar-water mixture. Season with salt, cover with sliced onions and tomatoes, and add black olives, bay leaf, and thyme. Cover and let stand in a cool place for 24 hours.

Transfer fish together with its marinade to a deep oven-proof dish. Bake in a moderate (300°) oven for 1 hour, basting frequently. Just before serving, add to the juice the fresh black peppercorns and serve directly from the dish in which the fish was cooked. (*Serves 8.*)

Baked Fish in Foil

(PESTE AL BASTRU)

Rumania

1 fish per person (red mullet or fresh herring)	1 tablespoon cooking oil
	3 thin slices of lemon
Salt	1 tablespoon butter
Freshly ground black pepper	2 teaspoons chopped chives

Allow 1 fish per person. Wash, scale, and clean out the insides of the fish but leave it whole. Rub with salt, sprinkle with pepper, and brush over with oil. Cut out aluminum foil in rectangular shape, place fish in the middle, cover with lemon slices, and dot with small pieces of butter, and the chives. Fold over the two sides of foil, tuck in well at the edges as if making a neat parcel, taking care that no juice should escape while cooking. Preheat oven to 300°, then reduce to moderate (250°), and bake fish for exactly 20 minutes. Carefully open the parcel, slip out fish on a preheated plate and pour the juice over it.
(Serves 1.)

Baked Whole Carp (or Cod)

(SARAN NA PRECANSKI NACIN)

Yugoslavia

This is one of the most tasteful ways to present a whole fish.
The original is a Serbian dish, ideal for carp, since it is a
fatty fish. But I have successfully prepared it with river cod
and with the Mediterranean *dentice*.

4 tablespoons butter	Salt
1 whole carp (or river cod or any good-sized fish)	1 tablespoon flour
	1 pound potatoes
5 slices bacon (or strips of larding bacon)	½ cup sour cream
1 teaspoon Hungarian sweet red paprika	

Butter well the sides and bottom of a deep baking dish. Place a
rack large enough to hold the fish inside without the fish
actually touching the pan.

Having washed, scaled, and cleaned fish, make incisions
crosswise, about an inch apart and deep enough for insertion
of strips of bacon without actually cutting fish up in slices,
alternating bacon with small dots of butter. (This method is
common when fish calls for larding and buttering.)

Blend the paprika with the salt and the flour. Peel potatoes and slice thinly in discs. Lay potatoes on the bottom
of the baking dish underneath the rack on which you have
placed the larded fish. Start baking it in a moderate (350°)
oven for 10 minutes. Now dust the fish with the flour-paprika
mixture, reduce heat of oven to 300° and continue baking for
another 10 minutes. Pour some of the sour cream on and

test potatoes, which should be almost cooked. Again increase temperature of oven to 350° to allow fish to become crisp and golden. Pour on rest of the sour cream and let bake for another 5 minutes.

Serve fish garnished with its own potatoes.

(*Serves 4–6.*)

Cod in Sour Cream

(SOM U MILERAMU)

Yugoslavia

1 *pound fresh or frozen cod fillets (or medium-sized river cod)*
Salt
4 *peppercorns*
½ *red onion*
1 *bay leaf*
Sprig *of parsley*

Peel of ½ lemon
½ *cup dry white wine*
6 *anchovies (pickled in brine or canned)*
2 *teaspoons flour*
¾ *cup sour cream*
1 *tablespoon butter*

Put fish in a saucepan and cover with cold water to which you add the salt, peppercorns, onion, bay leaf, parsley and lemon peel, together with a half cup of dry white wine. Boil for 6 minutes, drain but retain the cooking liquid. Clean anchovies and chop them very finely. Arrange fish fillets or whole fish in a buttered ovenproof dish, sprinkle with chopped anchovies. Blend the flour with the sour cream and dilute with the strained fish-liquid. Pour this sauce over the fish, dot with small pieces of butter and bake in moderate (350°) oven for 10 to 15 minutes.

(*Serves 4.*)

Trout in Tokay-Type Wine

(PISZTRANG TOKAJI BORBAN)

Hungary

4 medium-sized trout
   (1 for each person)
1¼ cups Tokay wine (or
   sweet sauterne or
   Madeira)
1 bay leaf
3–4 peppercorns

½ pickled black walnut,
   chopped (optional)
Salt
1 tablespoon flour
1½ tablespoons butter
Juice of ½ lemon

Clean trout but do not remove head or tail. In a saucepan put the wine, bay leaf, peppercorns, and the chopped walnut (optional). Bring this to boil and let it reduce by half of its original quantity. Add salt.

Brown the flour in butter, carefully dilute while stirring all the time with the wine, and keep barely *simmering*. Poach fish in this sauce for 8 minutes, taking care that the heat should be very gentle. If necessary, thin down sauce with a few spoonfuls of cold bouillon.

Just before serving, squeeze the lemon juice over fish. (*Serves 4.*)

Baked Stuffed Fish

(TOLTOTT HAL)

Hungary

1 fair-sized fish weighing 2–3 pounds	2 slices bacon, chopped
3 slices white bread, soaked in milk	4 anchovies, chopped
Very little salt	2 teaspoons chopped parsley
Freshly ground pepper	½ teaspoon Hungarian sweet red paprika
½ cup chopped raw mushrooms	2 tablespoons butter
	½ cup sour cream

Use a whole fish (fresh or sea-water) and leave on head and tail. Wash, scale, and clean. Fill the open cavity with the following stuffing:

In a mixing bowl put the bread, previously soaked in milk and then well drained. Season with salt, pepper, add the mushrooms, bacon, anchovies, and parsley, and work into a smooth paste. Fill fish with this mixture and sew up the opening.

Place fish in a well-buttered ovenproof dish, dust top with paprika and dot with small pieces of butter. Start baking it in a moderate (350°) oven for 10 minutes. Reduce heat to 250° and pour on the sour cream. Keep basting and bake for another 25 minutes. Serve garnished with the stuffing and boiled potatoes.

(Serves 4–6.)

Carp in Red Wine

(KARPF IM ROTWEIN)

Austria

1 carp (or any whole fish weighing about 2 pounds)	1 bay leaf
	1 teaspoon chopped parsley
	Sprig of thyme
2 cups dry red wine	3–4 mushroom caps or
Freshly ground black pepper	button mushrooms
	2 tablespoons butter
Salt	1 teaspoon flour

Cut fish crosswise but not through into strips one and a half inches wide. Place in a saucepan and pour the red wine over it. Add pepper, salt, bay leaf, parsley, thyme, and mushroom caps. Bring to boil, then reduce heat and let simmer very gently for 10 minutes. Carefully transfer fish to a warm serving platter and quickly prepare its sauce as follows:

Heat butter in a frying pan and fry flour till it is golden. Carefully strain over it the wine in which the fish was cooked and stir until sauce thickens. Pour this over the fish and decorate with the mushroom caps.

(*Serves* 4.)

Fish Casserole

(RIBA MUSSAKA)

Bulgaria

1 large red onion	Fat for deep-frying
3 fresh tomatoes	eggplants
3–4 tablespoons cooking oil	Freshly ground black
1 pound salted codfish	pepper
(or frozen cod fillets)	1 teaspoon Hungarian
3 large eggplants	sweet red paprika
Salt	3 eggs
Flour to dust over eggplants	

Finely chop the onion and peel and quarter tomatoes. In a frying pan heat the oil and fry the onion till golden. Add the codfish, cut into cubes, and the tomatoes. Cover and let stew for 15 minutes.

Slice eggplants in quarter-inch-thick pieces. Sprinkle with salt and let stand in a covered bowl for an hour. Dry thoroughly and coat with flour on both sides. Heat fat in a deep fryer and quickly fry eggplants till golden and crisp. Drain.

Butter a deep ovenproof casserole and make layers first of the fried eggplants, then the fish stew, then again eggplants. Season in between with very little salt, plenty of freshly ground black pepper and a little paprika. The top layer should be eggplant. Put casserole in a moderate (350°) oven and cook for half an hour. Beat eggs as if for an omelet (add a pinch of salt), and pour this mixture over the top of the *mussaka*. Return to oven to set. Eat hot or cold.

(Serves 4–6.)

Fish Stew Balkan Style

(RIBA GIVETSCH)

Bulgaria

Fish in Bulgaria is scarce and today's tourist, unless vacationing in a Black Sea resort, would seldom get fish served inland in restaurants. During Lent, Bulgarians would utilize canned tuna or salt cod to prepare a very tasty stew with fresh (or canned) green peppers and potatoes.

1 *pound salt cod (or canned tuna)*	1 *pound potatoes, thinly sliced*
4 *tablespoons oil*	Salt
2 *onions, chopped*	Freshly ground black pepper
6 *large green peppers (or canned peppers), seeded, chopped*	2 *tablespoons chopped parsley*
6 *medium-sized tomatoes, peeled, quartered*	

Cut fish into bite-sized pieces. Heat oil in a deep saucepan with a tight-fitting lid and fry onions till golden. Add the fish, the green peppers, the tomatoes, and the potatoes. Season carefully with salt and more generously with black pepper. Sprinkle with chopped parsley.

Put lid over the saucepan and on top of the stove (or some prefer it in a very low, 250°, oven) begin stewing at a gentle heat, without adding any water to it.

Stew for 1 hour or until all the vegetable juices have evaporated and the stew is thick and not watery.

(*Serves 6.*)

Fish in Gelatin

(HALKOCSONYA)

Hungary

This dish comes from Transylvania, which before the First World War belonged to Hungary and is now part of Rumania. When carp is available, it is usually made with that fish, but I have prepared it even with frozen whiting and had very satisfactory results.

2 *cups water*	2 *red onions, finely*
2 *tablespoons white wine*	*sliced*
vinegar	2 *large carrots, sliced*
1 *to 1½ pounds fish*	1 *bay leaf*
fillets or steaks	1 *envelope gelatin*
(*whiting, cod, etc.*)	1 *teaspoon Hungarian*
Salt	*sweet red paprika*
6–8 *peppercorns*	

Boil water with vinegar and immediately pour over the fish fillets. Add salt, peppercorns, onion, carrots, and bay leaf. Cover and let stand for a few hours. Now transfer fish and liquid to a saucepan and gently boil, without lid on, for 20 minutes. Carefully remove fish fillets and arrange in a large china dish deep enough to hold a pint or so of liquid.

Dissolve gelatin in a little cold water, add paprika to color it. Strain the fish liquid through a fine sieve, bring it again to boil. Mix with gelatin, pour over the fish, and let set in the refrigerator.

(*Serves 4–6.*)

Danube Fish Soup

(HALASZLE)

Hungary

The genuine Hungarian *halászlé* is prepared by fishermen on the banks of the river in a kettle suspended above an open fire. This soup is a cross between a fish stew and a soup, and in Budapest restaurants situated along the Danube quai specialize in it. The choice of fish is one of the most important parts of this dish: there must be at least one kind of fatty fish, like river cod or carp. Then perch and a host of small fish are added for the base. Live fish are used by fishermen who cut them open over the kettle with a sharp knife, letting the blood out, which gives the soup its rich flavor.

However, the method, whether one uses river fish or a selection of sea fish, is always the same. Instead of the kettle a saucepan and kitchen stove can be used, unless one happens to camp alongside a river in summer or has an open-air barbecue in one's garden.

½ pound carp	Salt
½ pound river cod	2 teaspoons Hungarian
½ pound perch	sweet red paprika
1 medium-sized red onion, finely sliced	1–2 green peppers

Remove tail, head, fins of fish and put them in a deep saucepan together with the onion, and salt. Cover with cold water and bring to boil. Keep boiling without a lid for 20 minutes, then strain and discard bones.

Cut fish into inch-thick strips crosswise, and pour the fish stock over it. Season with paprika and add the sliced green peppers. Bring to boil, let simmer for 15 minutes, without ever touching the fish to avoid flaking. Serve hot. (*Serves 8.*)

Crawfish Soup

(KREBSENSUPPE)

Austria

In countries like Austria, Hungary and France, where in season (from May until September) crawfish (*écrevisse*) are found in rivers, this soup is treated with great respect. Live crawfish are used, boiled first in lightly salted water together with a few caraway seeds, parsley, peppercorns. After 8 minutes the crawfish turns a bright red in color. The shell is pounded in a mortar and the pulp passed through a fine wire sieve: this is called the crawfish butter and is used for seasoning.

1½ dozen live crawfish	*4 tablespoons dry white*
Salt	*wine*
1 teaspoon caraway seed	*1 egg yolk*
4 peppercorns	*¼ cup fresh cream*
2 stalks fresh parsley	*Dash of cognac*
2 tablespoons butter	

Boil water in a large saucepan and drop in crawfish. Season with salt, caraway seed, peppercorns and parsley. Cook for 8 minutes. Take out crawfish and strain liquid, which you retain.

Heat half the butter in a saucepan. Take out crawfish meat from claws and tails. Pound shell in a mortar or put in an electric blender. Press pulp through a wire sieve.

Add wine to liquid in which you boiled crawfish. Reheat and put back the meat from shells. In a mixing bowl blend together the strained pulp of the shells, egg yolk, and cream. Add this, together with a dash of cognac, to the soup and serve immediately, with the rest of the butter mixed in.

Note: This recipe can be made with frozen lobster, crab, or other shellfish. Instead of water use canned bouillon.
(*Serves 4–6.*)

Dalmatian Fish Soup

(DALMATINSKA RIBLJA CORBA)

Yugoslavia

2 *pounds mixed fish*	*Salt*
(*fresh-water or*	*Coarsely ground black*
salt-water)	*pepper*
4 *ripe tomatoes*	*Sprig of parsley*
3 *cloves garlic*	1 *teaspoon mixed herbs*
1 *green pepper*	(*orégano, thyme, basil*)
4 *tablespoons cooking oil*	6 *cups water*

Use whole fish preferably (mullet, herring, sardine), wash, scale, but leave on heads and tails.

Peel and quarter tomatoes, finely chop garlic, and dice green pepper. Heat the oil in a heavy iron skillet, lightly fry garlic, and add tomatoes, pepper, together with seasoning: very little salt, freshly ground black pepper, the sprig of parsley, and the herbs. Reduce flame and fry, stirring all ingredients with a wooden spoon.

After 10 minutes, put fish on top of this vegetable pulp and cover with cold water. Bring to boil, reduce, and let cook without a lid on for 20 minutes. Serve fish with the soup in deep bowls.
(*Serves 6.*)

Blue Trout

(FORELLEN BLAU)

Austria

This classical recipe would mainly interest trout fishermen or those gourmets who have traveled widely in the mountainous regions of Austria, Switzerland, the High Tatras, and the Carpathians. The secret of the blue trout is to use freshly caught, still live fish that must be killed by one stroke on a chopping block in the kitchen. Only the insides are removed: the skin must be carefully preserved.

2 cups water	4–6 peppercorns
Very little salt	3 tablespoons diced carrot
3 tablespoons wine vinegar	2 sprigs parsley
3 tablespoons finely chopped onion	1 river trout per person
	Melted butter served separately

In a saucepan bring the salted water to boil, to which is added the vinegar, onion, peppercorns, carrot, and parsley. This stock, which in German is called *Brühe*, must be boiled uncovered for 15 minutes before you put the trout in. As soon as fish turns blue, turn off the heat and leave fish in stock for exactly 15 minutes longer.

Carefully take fish out so as not to bruise the skin and serve with melted butter. Boiled new potatoes with parsley are usual accompaniment.

(*Serves 1.*)

Tyrolean Trout

(FORELLEN TYROLER ART)

Austria

6 *trout*	*Finely sifted breadcrumbs*
Flour	*Butter for frying*
Salt	*Slices of lemon*
Pepper	TARTARE SAUCE (*see below*)
1 or 2 eggs, beaten	

Use only small-sized river trout for this dish. Clean out insides, and bend the fish in a way that their tail can be inserted in their mouth. Do not skin or remove bones, but leave them whole. Season flour with salt and pepper. Beat the eggs as if for an omelet. Spread breadcrumbs thickly on a plate or thick paper. Roll fish well in seasoned flour, taking care to cover all over. Now dip into beaten egg and immediately coat with breadcrumbs. Heat butter (or any cooking fat) in a frying pan. A deep-fryer is not recommended, but fat should be used generously in order to prevent crumbs from sticking to the pan. When fat is hot, fry fish quickly on all sides to a crisp, golden brown. Drain thoroughly on absorbent paper.

Serve with lemon slices and offer a TARTARE SAUCE separately (this is a mayonnaise to which you add some chopped gherkins, capers, and olives).

(*Serves 6.*)

Fish Steaks Admiral Style

(FOGAS ADMIRALIS MODRA)

Hungary

In Hungary, the king of all fresh-water fish, the Lake Balaton *fogas*, is used for this recipe. *Fogas (Lucioperca sandra var. Fogas balatonicus* for experts in Latin) is prized for its soft white flesh and delicate, sweetish flavor.

8 *fish steaks (river cod, pike, carp)*	3 *tablespoons butter*
Salt	1 *cup small shrimp (frozen may be used)*
5 *or* 6 *peppercorns*	*Dash of cognac*
1 *glass white wine*	2 *tablespoons flour*
Juice of 1 *lemon*	*Grated Parmesan cheese*
Sprig of parsley	

Wash and dry the fish steaks thoroughly, allowing 2 small cutlets per person. Butter an ovenproof dish well (one that can go to the table) and place the steaks in it. Lightly salt, sprinkle with peppercorns, and moisten with wine and lemon juice. Add parsley. Cover and poach in moderate (350°) oven for 15 minutes. Meanwhile, in a saucepan heat the butter and fry the shrimp for a few minutes. Pour on cognac (ignite if possible) then blend in the flour. Moisten with the poaching liquid of the fish, bring sauce to the correct thickness.

Pour this sauce back over the steaks, sprinkle with grated Parmesan cheese, and brown under the broiler.
(*Serves* 4.)

Baked Fish with Asparagus

(FISCH GRATIN MIT SPARGELN)

Austria

1 whole fish, 2–3 pounds	1 cup asparagus pieces
Salt	(canned)
2 tablespoons butter	Black pepper
2 tablespoons flour	1 egg yolk, beaten
½ cup milk	Grated Parmesan cheese
½ cup fish stock (or	Breadcrumbs
canned bouillon)	

Boil fish first in salted water for 10 minutes. Strain and retain the liquid.

Put the whole fish in a well-buttered ovenproof dish and pour over it the following sauce:

Heat the butter and add the flour, stir while pouring on milk and fish stock (or canned bouillon). Let sauce boil gently to thicken (the same as for making a white sauce). Add the asparagus pieces, season with pepper and if necessary a little more salt. Off the fire mix in the yolk of an egg and a generous helping of grated Parmesan cheese. Dust with fine breadcrumbs.

With this sauce the fish should bake in a moderate (350°) oven for another 10 minutes.

(Serves 4–6.)

Fish Fillets with Mushrooms

(HAL GOMBAVAL)

Hungary

4 medium-sized potatoes
2 tablespoons butter
Flour
Salt
Black pepper
1 pound filleted fish
  (whiting, flounder,
  sole, etc.)
1 cup chopped
  mushrooms

2 teaspoons chopped
  parsley
1 tablespoon flour
¼ cup light cream
1 cup canned bouillon
  (or meat or vegetable
  stock)
Juice of ½ lemon

Peel and halve the potatoes, parboil them. Butter a deep, oven-proof baking dish that can also go to the table. Season flour with salt and pepper and dip fish fillets in it. Arrange fish in the center of the dish and surround with the potatoes. Sprinkle with the chopped mushrooms, parsley.

Blend 1 tablespoon of flour with the cream and mix with the bouillon or stock and lemon juice. Pour this sauce over the fish and the potatoes. Bake in first a moderate (300°) oven for 5 minutes, then reduce to 200° and cook for 25 minutes or until the potatoes, which take longer to cook, are tender. (*Serves 4.*)

Fish on the Spit
(NYARSON SULT HAL)
Hungary

In Hungary, fishermen cook the small Danube fish on a spit. Using wooden skewers, they thread the perch, pike, and sterlet on it and grill it barbecue fashion over an open fire. I have done this fish barbecue with red mullets, fresh sardines, and whitings mixed. What's more, you needn't go into the garden if you have an electric spit attachment for your oven, or a rotisserie in the kitchen.

4 or 5 small fish per person
Slices bacon (or smoked larding bacon)
Salt
Hungarian sweet red paprika
Oil for brushing outside of fish
Tomatoes
Green peppers

Thread fish, alternating it with bacon, on a skewer. Sprinkle with very little salt, since bacon is salty, and some paprika. Use an ordinary kitchen brush to brush fish over with a little oil, otherwise they become too dry. Cook till fish is crisp and golden.

Serve with chopped fresh tomatoes and chopped green peppers. (*Serves 1.*)

Prawns (Scampi) in Brandy

(SKAMPI U BRANDIJU)

Yugoslavia

This dish can be found on the menus of first-class hotels along the Dalmatian coast. *Scampi*—Mediterranean prawns—are used for it; they are larger than our prawns.

3 tablespoons cooking oil or butter	Dash of brandy
2 cloves garlic, chopped	2 tablespoons flour
1 tablespoon chopped parsley	½ cup canned bouillon (or meat or vegetable stock)
1½ pounds prawns (or shrimp)	¼ cup dry white wine
Flour	Coarsely ground black pepper
Salt	

If possible, this should be made with uncooked prawns. However, if those are unobtainable, use ready-cooked ones—in an emergency even the frozen prawns.

In a shallow iron skillet heat the oil or butter. Fry the garlic and the parsley for a few seconds.

Coat prawns with flour and a little salt. Fry in the garlic fat until crisp and golden on all sides. Pour on a dash of brandy, ignite, and swill out pan.

Blend in 2 tablespoons of flour and moisten with bouillon and wine. Season with plenty of pepper. Let cook, stirring all the time, for 5 more minutes. Serve directly from the frying pan.

(Serves 4.)

Prawns (Scampi) in Aspic

(SKAMPI U ASPIKU)

Yugoslavia

This dish comes from a retired sea captain who lives in Rijeka, a large Adriatic port. Rijeka was called Fiume until the end of the First World War. It belonged to the Austro-Hungarian monarchy, and later by the Italians, who ceded it to Yugoslavia in 1947. This is a very attractive dish for a cold buffet. Instead of the Mediterranean scampi, you can use prawns, fresh or ready-cooked as well.

1 envelope gelatin	1 pound prawns
2 cups water	2 cups Russian salad
Juice of ½ lemon	(see below)
2 tablespoons Madeira	2 hard-cooked eggs
wine	Sprigs of fresh parsley

If fresh prawns are used, boil them for 8 minutes in salted water to which a teaspoon of caraway seed and a sprig of parsley are added. Remove shells.

Prepare an aspic with the gelatin and the water, flavor it with fresh lemon juice and the Madeira wine. Rinse out a round Charlotte mold with cold water and half-fill with the liquid aspic. Let it set in the refrigerator, and when firm, arrange the shelled prawns on top. Pour over them the remaining of melted aspic and return to the refrigerator to set thoroughly.

Unmold and arrange the Russian salad (mixed, diced, cooked vegetables, gherkins, potatoes dressed with a thick mayonnaise) in the middle of the aspic ring. Decorate with egg slices and sprigs of fresh parsley. (Serves 6–8.)

Crawfish (Lobster, Prawn) Paprika

(RAKPORKOLT)

Hungary

2 tablespoons butter	Salt
½ small onion, grated	1 tablespoon flour
1 teaspoon Hungarian	½ cup canned bouillon
sweet red paprika	(or stock)
1½ pounds shelled	¼ cup sour cream
crawfish, lobster, or	Boiled rice garnish
prawns (cooked, fresh	
or frozen)	

(If fresh crawfish, lobster, or prawns are used, retain the cooking liquid and use this for the sauce.) Heat the butter in a shallow iron skillet and fry the grated onion until it is golden. Blend in the paprika. Having cooked and shelled your shellfish, cut the lobster up in bite-sized pieces but leave the prawns or crawfish whole.

Fry the onion and paprika with the shellfish for a few minutes. Add salt to taste. Now blend in the flour and moisten with bouillon (or stock). Stir, bringing sauce to the correct thickness, which should take about 5 minutes. Lastly, off the fire, add the sour cream. Serve garnished with boiled rice. (Serves 4.)

Crawfish (Prawn or Lobster) Rice

(KREBSENRISOTTO)

Austria

A highly praised dish on the menu of Vienna's Hotel Imperial, the meeting place of all the chic people in the Kaiserstadt before the war. At the Hotel Imperial the chef used crawfish tails in season and for the sauce the crawfish butter. I have frequently prepared this dish with cooked lobster or prawns (even with frozen shellfish).

4 tablespoons butter	½ cup heavy cream
1 cup uncooked, long-grain rice	½ cup cooked or frozen peas
1½ cups canned bouillon (meat or vegetable stock)	½ cup chopped button mushrooms
Salt	1½ teaspoons chopped parsley
Pepper	Grated Parmesan cheese
1½ cups cooked, shelled crawfish, prawns, or diced lobster	Hot melted butter
1 teaspoon Hungarian sweet red paprika	

Heat 3 tablespoons of the butter in a saucepan and dry-fry the rice first, taking care not to brown it. Pour on the canned bouillon (or stock), add, if necessary, salt and pepper, bring to boil, then reduce immediately. Let rice steam under a tightly fitting lid for 10 to 12 minutes or until all the liquid is absorbed.

Meanwhile, in a separate frying pan, heat the remaining butter and add the diced lobster or shelled prawns. Sprinkle with paprika. Remove from heat, add the thick cream.

Now add the cooked peas, mushrooms, chopped fresh parsley, and the shellfish in its sauce to the separately cooked rice. Blend well together, but take care not to bruise the rice grains. Sprinkle generously with grated cheese and serve hot. Serve melted butter separately.

(*This dish, as a first course, should serve 6 persons amply.*)

Carp Steaks (Fish Cutlets)

(SMAZENY KAPR)

Czechoslovakia

Carp, river cod, sometimes pike, and, in the Slovakian parts, trout are the fish preferred in households all over Czechoslovakia. Carp cutlets fried in breadcrumbs are a traditional Christmas Eve dinner. Fresh salmon done this way is also very good as a substitute.

4 carp steaks (or any fish cutlets)	Oil or fat for semideep frying
Salt	Freshly ground black pepper
Flour	
1 egg	Lemon slices
Finely sifted breadcrumbs	Potato salad for garnish

Wash and dry the fish cutlets. Salt and dust well with flour. Beat the egg and dip cutlets in it. Roll them in breadcrumbs and fry them in oil until golden and crisp on both sides. Season with pepper. Garnish with lemon slices and serve a cold potato salad separately.

(*Serves 4.*)

Carp Steaks (Fish Cutlets) in Paprika

(KAPR NA PAPRICE)

Czechoslovakia

<table>
<tr><td>2 tablespoons bacon fat
(or cooking oil)</td><td>2 tablespoons flour
1 cup canned bouillon</td></tr>
<tr><td>1 small onion, finely
chopped</td><td>(or water)
Salt</td></tr>
<tr><td>1 teaspoon Hungarian
sweet red paprika</td><td>4–6 fish steaks (carp,
cod, fresh salmon)</td></tr>
</table>

Heat the fat (or oil) in a frying pan and fry the onion until it is golden. Blend in the paprika together with the flour. Stir and fry for a few seconds, then dilute with cold bouillon (or water). Add salt.

Place the steaks in this sauce, reduce heat, and let cook, uncovered for 5 minutes on one side and another 5 minutes on the other. If necessary, thin down sauce with a little more water or bouillon. Serve with mashed or boiled potatoes. (Serves 4.)

Carp in Black Sauce

(KAPR NA CERNO)

Czechoslovakia

This is an elaborate and very highly regarded dish, served for Christmas. The sauce has a distinct sweet-and-sour taste. As a rule, a large, whole carp was used, with the blood carefully

extracted and added to the sauce. I have prepared it successfully with cod, turbot, large perch, or the Mediterranean
dorado.

2 tablespoons butter
½ onion, minced
1 cup mixed diced
  carrots and celery
Salt
8 peppercorns
1 bay leaf
1 teaspoon mixed herbs
  (thyme, orégano, sage)
½ cup beer
Juice of 1 lemon
3 tablespoons wine
  vinegar

½ cup red wine
2 teaspoons sugar
½ cup chopped walnuts
6 dried prunes, chopped
3 tablespoons seeded
  raisins
2 tablespoons plum jam
8–10 fish cutlets
3 tablespoons blanched
  and chopped almonds

Prepare the sauce in which to poach the fish as follows: in a
saucepan heat butter and lightly fry onion and diced carrots and
celery. Add salt, peppercorns, bay leaf, and mixed herbs,
moisten with a little cold water. Cover and steam for 15
minutes. Put through a sieve, add beer, lemon juice, vinegar and
the wine, together with the sugar. Mix in the chopped walnuts,
chopped prunes, raisins, and plum jam. (If sauce is too thick,
add a few tablespoons of cold water or canned bouillon.)
Poach the cutlets in this sauce at gentle heat without a cover
for 15 minutes. Serve, with the almonds strewn on top.
(*Serves 6.*)

Fish Baked in Bread

(PETSCHENE RIBA)

Bulgaria

A unique but exquisite way to prepare a whole fish, not unlike the ham which is baked in bread dough. In country kitchens in Bulgaria, fish prepared in this way is generally sent to the baker's oven or done in the old-fashioned stoves heated with wood.

1½ pounds bread dough or pizza dough	Salt
1 whole fish (fresh-water or sea-water) weighing at least 3–4 pounds	4–5 tablespoons oil 4–5 tablespoons bacon fat (melted)

Use a yeasty dough, either from the ready-mix package or according to a reliable homemade bread recipe. Divide dough into 2 parts and roll out to pizza-thickness (slightly less than a half inch). Wash, scale, and clean out insides of fish, rub with salt. Mix oil and melted bacon fat.

Place fish in the center of the divided half of the rolled-out dough, brush all over with the mixed fat. Lay the second part of dough on top, press down the edges firmly. It should resemble a rectangular pie.

Brush top with the rest of the fat and put in a moderate (350°) oven to start. After 5 minutes turn oven down to 250° and bake until crisp and golden. The slower you bake it the tastier both the bread and the fish will be. (Serves 6.)

Baked Fish (Carp or Other)

(PETSCHEN SCHARAN)

Bulgaria

The fish is prepared here according to an old Turkish recipe, which was adapted to Bulgarian kitchens. (In Bulgaria, like in most countries in Central and Eastern Europe, carp is the commonest of all the river fish.)

1 whole fish weighing 3–4 pounds	1 bay leaf
½ cup cooking oil	Salt
4 or 5 medium-sized onions, finely chopped	6 peppercorns
1 cup chopped walnuts	½ cup canned bouillon (or stock)
1 cup sultana raisins	1 dry bread roll (or 2 slices toasted white bread)
Peel of ½ lemon, chopped	

Wash, clean, and leave the fish whole. Put oil in a saucepan, fry the onion until it is transparent. Add the chopped walnuts, sultanas, lemon peel, and bay leaf. Season with salt and peppercorns, moisten with the canned bouillon. Cover and let steam for 15 minutes. Mix with crumbed bread roll.

Grease an oblong ovenproof casserole. Line with half of the onion-walnut mixture. Place fish on top and cover with the remaining half of the mixture. Bake in a 300° oven for half an hour, then reduce heat to 150° and continue for 10 more minutes. Serve hot or cold.

(Serves 4–6.)

POULTRY

Turkey with Sauerkraut

(PODVARAK)

Yugoslavia

An original way to prepare the tender young turkey. This is a popular dish in northern Yugoslavia.

1 tender young turkey about 6 pounds	1 parsnip
	1 stalk celery
Salt	Sprig of parsley
6–8 peppercorns	Fat for greasing casserole
2 cloves garlic	1½ pounds fresh
1 onion	sauerkraut (or canned)
1 bay leaf	5 slices bacon
2 carrots	

In a large saucepan, with enough cold water to cover it, bring turkey to boil, together with seasoning, salt, and peppercorns. Add the garlic, whole onion, and the bay leaf, allow to simmer gently, covered, for 1 hour.

Now add the carrots cut into halves, the parsnip, the celery and the sprig of parsley, boil for another 15 minutes. Retain the cooking liquid.

Cut the turkey into serving portions. In a deep ovenproof casserole, well greased with cooking fat, place the sauerkraut. Taste and add salt if necessary. Moisten with one and a half cups of the cooking liquid for boiling turkey. Arrange the pieces of meat on top, cover with bacon. Bake in a moderate (350°) oven for 35 minutes. (*Serves 6–8.*)

Serbian Chicken Stew

(PILECA CORBA)

Yugoslavia

This stew—the *čorba*—is half soup, half stew, and is served with plenty of gravy.

1 large boiling fowl	3 green peppers, sliced
3 medium-sized onions	3–4 fresh tomatoes,
2 tablespoons cooking fat	quartered
or oil	½ small green cabbage
1 teaspoon Hungarian	4 medium-sized potatoes,
sweet red paprika	peeled, quartered
Salt	
Freshly ground black	
pepper	

Cut chicken into serving portions (6 to 8 pieces) and finely chop onions. Heat fat in a stewing pot and fry the onion in fat until it is golden. Sprinkle with the paprika and put the chicken pieces in and lightly fry for a few minutes. Now cover with cold water (about 5 cups), season with salt and pepper, and bring to boil. Cover, reduce heat, and allow to simmer for half an hour.

Core the green peppers and cut into long strips, quarter the tomatoes. Roughly shred the cabbage. Add these to the stew and continue cooking for another 15 minutes. Now add the potatoes and cook for half an hour more.
(*Serves 6.*)

Chicken Paprika

(PAPRIKAS CSIRKE)

Hungary

In general, abroad, chicken paprika means a stew with a red paprika gravy. In Hungary there are two distinct variations, however. The one where the gravy contains sour cream is the commonly known chicken paprika. The other dish, where the gravy is not thickened with the cream, is *pörkölt*. The same distinction is made with the veal paprika and the veal stew, or *pörkölt*, the latter being without cream.

1 stewing chicken	Salt
2 tablespoons bacon fat	2 tablespoons flour
1 medium-sized red onion, finely chopped	1 cup canned bouillon (or water)
1–2 teaspoons Hungarian sweet red paprika	½ cup sour cream

Cut up the chicken into 6 to 8 pieces. In a stewing pot heat the bacon fat and fry the onion until it is golden. Sprinkle with the red paprika and brown the chicken pieces first in the fat. Now add salt, cover with the lid, and greatly reduce heat. Let chicken begin to stew in its own juice for at least 15 minutes. Depending how tough your chicken, keep stewing, moistening it occasionally with a few spoonfuls of cold stock or water.

When the meat is tender, remove from pot and keep warm. Blend in flour with the gravy and dilute, stirring with a wooden spoon, with the bouillon or water. Let it cook gently, uncovered, till the sauce is thick. Put back the chicken pieces, reheat. Remove from heat, just before serving add the sour cream. Never boil with the cream!

In Hungary chicken paprika is served with small EGG DUMP-LINGS, called *noki*. Another suitable garnish is boiled rice. (*Serves 6.*)

Viennese Spring Chicken

(HEURIGES BACKHUHN)

Austria

One of the greatest and best-known specialties of the Viennese kitchen, these tender spring chickens are awaited with great eagerness each year. Accompanied with the first fresh lettuce salad, and eaten in an elegant restaurant, at home on Sundays, or in little pubs around Grinzing or Döbling, spring chicken is an unforgettable experience, just like the opera.

2 very young, tender, small fryers	Finely sifted, homemade breadcrumbs
1 or 2 eggs	Oil or bacon fat for semideep frying
Salt	
Flour	

Cut up chickens (they should be so young that you may break them easily at the joints) into 8 pieces each—the leg into 2 parts, wings apart, breast sliced lengthwise into 2. *Do not remove bones!*

Beat the egg and season with salt. Dry the pieces of chicken thoroughly, coat them with flour, and dip quickly into beaten egg. Lastly roll in breadcrumbs.

Deep fry to crisp golden brown. Drain on absorbent paper and serve at once.

(*Serves 6.*)

Chicken in Tomato Sauce

(PARADAJZ SOS SA PILETINOM)

Yugoslavia

1 stewing fowl	Few sprigs of basil (or
4 slices bacon	pinch of orégano)
2 cloves garlic	2 tablespoons flour
1 pound fresh (or canned)	1 cup canned bouillon
tomatoes	1 teaspoon sugar
Salt	Juice of ½ lemon
Freshly ground black	
pepper	

Cut chicken into 6 to 8 pieces. Chop bacon and crush garlic. Fry bacon first, then, in the fat, the garlic, and lastly the chicken pieces. Reduce heat, cover, and let stew (without any additional liquid) for 15 minutes.

Peel and quarter tomatoes and add to stew. Season with salt, pepper, and basil (or orégano). Continue cooking until meat is tender, about another hour. Remove pieces of chicken, stir in the flour and cook gravy, moistened with the bouillon. Add sugar, put gravy through a wire sieve. Put back the meat, reheat thoroughly, and lastly, off the fire, add the lemon juice. (Serves 6.)

Chicken Stew

(EINGEMACHTES HUHN)

Austria

This chicken stew tastes best in springtime, with the arrival of the first fresh vegetables. Kohlrabies, when in season, and before they turn hard and woody, lend their distinct flavor to all Austrian stews, called *Eingemachtes*.

1 stewing fowl	2 cups canned bouillon
3 tablespoons butter or	(or stock)
bacon fat	Salt
2 young carrots, diced	Ground pepper
2 tender kohlrabies, diced	1 cup fresh (or frozen)
2 teaspoons chopped	peas
parsley	2 tablespoons flour
2 or 3 lumps sugar	

Cut chicken into serving pieces. Heat the butter in a stewing pan, fry the chicken pieces on all sides. Remove, and put in the carrots, kohlrabies, and parsley, together with the lump sugar. Cover and steam, letting carrots caramelize to induce more flavor.

Add the chicken pieces to the vegetables, moisten with half the bouillon or stock. Season with salt and pepper to taste. Stew under cover until meat is almost tender. Add the fresh green peas (or frozen) peas and finish cooking for 6 more minutes.

Blend in the flour, stir, and fry with the pulp vegetables and dilute with the remaining bouillon. Bring to boil, without lid, and let the gravy thicken, but do not allow it to get too thick. This stew must always be served with plenty of gravy. (*Serves 6.*)

Duckling with Red Cabbage

(KACHNAS CERVENYM-ZELIM)

Czechoslovakia

1 tart, green cooking apple	Freshly ground black pepper
1 small orange	1 small red cabbage
2 tablespoons chopped bacon	Bacon fat
1 duck about 3 pounds	1 bay leaf
Salt	Peppercorns

Peel, core, and quarter the apple. Peel and slice the orange. Fill the inside of the duck with the fruit and the chopped bacon. Rub with coarse salt and sprinkle with freshly ground black pepper.

Roast in a moderate (350°) oven without any fat added. Baste frequently with its own fat. Cooking time should be approximately 1 hour for a young duck. When meat is tender, increase the heat of oven to 400° maximum and crisp the skin, which must be golden.

The Red Cabbage:

Finely shred the red cabbage and remove the hard white core. Sprinkle with salt and let it stand, covered, in an earthenware container for a few hours. Squeeze out dry (the longer the cabbage is allowed to stand, the more juice will form in the dish. If eaten raw as a salad, the cabbage should be made to stand in salt to soften overnight).

Heat in a deep saucepan a few tablespoonfuls of bacon fat. Put in cabbage, add a bay leaf, some peppercorns, but no water. Cover and steam at a gentle heat for three quarters of an hour. Serve hot.
(*Serves 4.*)

Capon in Wine

(KAPOUN VE VINE)

Czechoslovakia

Capon, the desexed fowl noted for its tender, plump flesh, is highly regarded as a delicacy in all Central European countries. Boiled with vegetables, it makes an excellent strong broth (bouillon) and connoisseurs appreciate its meat as much as they do a good cut of boiled beef.

1 capon about 5 pounds	*1 parsnip, sliced*
2 cups Riesling	*Sprig of parsley*
Salt	*2 tablespoons butter*
2–5 peppercorns	*2 tablespoons flour*
½ red onion (or 2 or 3 spring onions)	*2 anchovies, finely chopped*
2 carrots, sliced	*1 yolk egg*
1 stalk celery, chopped	*Juice of ½ lemon*

Set capon to boil in the wine and just enough cold water to cover it. Season with salt, peppercorns, cover and steam for 25 minutes. Now add the onion, carrots, celery, parsnip, and parsley and continue gently boiling until meat is tender—about 1 hour.

In a separate saucepan heat the butter and fry the flour till

golden. Strain over this about 2 cups of the cooking liquid of the capon, and, stirring steadily, bring sauce to a creamy thickness. Add anchovies. Cut up the capon into serving pieces, return to sauce and reheat. Blend the yolk of an egg with the lemon juice, and add to the sauce.
(*Serves 6.*)

Roast Goose

(JUNGE GANS, GEBRATEN)

Austria

The Austrian kitchen thinks especially highly of the young goose. In Hungary, where goose used to be fattened with a special regard to increasing the size of its liver—by force-feeding, which is no longer permitted—goose was often as big as a turkey and consequently needed a lot of cooking.

The large goose must always be steamed in a little water on top of the stove and only then placed in the oven to roast. This process is not required with the tender young goose or duck.

> 1 *young goose about 6 pounds*
> Salt
> *Fresh marjoram (or 1 teaspoonful dried)*
> 3 *or 4 tart cooking apples*

Clean, truss the goose, which should be seasoned with salt and marjoram and stuffed with unpeeled, cored, and quartered tart small apples.

The important factor is the roasting. It should be done very *slowly*, in a 325° oven. Cooking time is approximately 2½ hours, and the bird must be regularly basted with its own fat. (Sometimes one may add a few tablespoonfuls of cold water to the roasting pan.) Cut up and serve goose, with its own juice in a sauceboat. (Do not make a gravy for the goose—it is never done in Austria.)

The correct garnishes for goose are: cabbage salad; warm red or green cooked cabbage; stewed, unsweetened chestnuts; boiled potatoes; wild rice; stewed apples; stewed prunes. (Of course, only a choice of the garnishes should be served.) (*Serves* 6.)

Roast Stuffed Goose

(GUSKA PUNJENA PIRINOTOM)

Yugoslavia

1 large goose, 8–10
    pounds
4 tablespoons uncooked
    rice
1 cup chopped fresh
    mushrooms
2 cups cold water for
    steaming

2 cloves garlic, crushed
Salt
Freshly ground black
    pepper
2 tablespoons bacon fat

In a covered pan set the cleaned and trussed goose, which you
have previously stuffed with the rice-and-mushroom filling
(see below). Pour over it the 2 cups of cold water, add the
garlic, salt, and a little pepper. Cover and steam on top of the
stove over low heat for about 1 hour. Drain and put goose on
a rack inside a baking dish and transfer to a warm (but not
hot) (325°) oven. Roast, basting it regularly, until meat is
tender, about another 2½–3 hours.

The Stuffing:

In a saucepan heat the bacon fat, add chopped mushrooms,
cover and steam for 5 minutes. Add the uncooked rice, only
just cover with cold water. Gently boil covered for a further
6 minutes. Season with salt and black pepper. Put stuffing
inside goose. When serving, the goose should be cut up into
serving portions and the mushroom-rice offered as a garnish
around it.
(Serves 6.)

Chicken Rice

(PILAF)

Bulgaria

1 *medium-sized chicken*	1 *stalk celery, diced*
2 *or 3 extra sets of*	2 *parsnips, diced*
giblets	1 *cup uncooked rice*
Salt	2 *teaspoons chopped*
Freshly ground black	*parsley*
pepper	3 *or 4 tablespoons*
4–6 *small diced button*	*chicken fat or bacon*
onions	*fat (melted)*
2 *carrots, diced*	1 *cup sultana raisins*

Put the whole chicken and the cleaned giblets in a saucepan containing enough cold water to cover. Add salt, pepper, and small onions. Cover and bring to boil. Let simmer for half an hour. Add the carrots, celery, and parsnips and cook until meat is tender—about 1 more hour. Remove chicken and strain the liquid, which should be kept to use for the rice. Discard vegetables.

In a separate saucepan set the rice to boil with the chicken stock. The cooking should not take over 12 minutes, or until all the liquid is absorbed and the rice stands separated and fluffy. Sprinkle with chopped parsley.

Cut up the chicken in small portions. Dice the gizzards, cut up livers. Leave necks whole. Mix these ingredients together with the rice adding sultanas and also the melted chicken fat or bacon fat, but without cooking it. Do the mixing with a long wooden fork, to prevent breaking up rice.

(*Serves 6–8.*)

Chicken Liver Pâté

(MAJPASTETOM)

Hungary

1 pound chicken livers	Freshly ground black
(or pork or calf's liver)	pepper
Milk	Dash of brandy or sherry
4 tablespoons butter	½ cup canned bouillon
2 cloves garlic	2 slices white bread
Salt	Juice of 1 lemon

Cut livers up coarsely and cover with a little cold milk. Let stand for a few hours or overnight in the refrigerator.

In a heavy frying pan heat 1 tablespoon of the butter and lightly fry whole garlic. Discard garlic and put in the well-drained liver pieces. At strong heat fry briskly all over. This should take no more than 5 minutes. Now add salt, plenty of black pepper, and pour on brandy or sherry. When warmed, ignite and swill out pan. While livers are still warm, add the rest of the butter—off the fire—and the bouillon. Add the bread, previously soaked in a little milk and squeezed dry. Add lemon juice.

Put all these ingredients in an electric blender or rub through a wire sieve twice. Press *pâté* in a mold that you have rinsed out in cold water, keep in refrigerator until hard and well set. (Serves 8.)

Chicken in Sour Cream

(CSIRKE TEJFOLBEN)

Hungary

1 young frying chicken (or 4 chicken breasts)	1 bay leaf
Flour to coat chicken	1 sprig each of thyme, marjoram
1½ tablespoons butter	1½ teaspoons Hungarian sweet red paprika
Salt	1½ cups sour cream
Freshly ground black pepper	Juice of ½ lemon
2 sprigs of parsley	

Use only tender chicken pieces or chicken breasts for this dish. A very elegant meal can be had by serving chicken breasts like scallops in a creamy sauce, garnished with long-grain rice.

Cut up chicken into serving pieces, dry thoroughly, and dust well with flour. In a heavy iron skillet heat the butter and fry the chicken pieces until golden on all sides. Add salt, pepper, the parsley, bay leaf, thyme, and marjoram. Blend the paprika with the sour cream, which should then have a reddish color. Pour this cream over the chicken, cover skillet with a lid, and let simmer, very, very gently for about 20 minutes, or until the meat is tender. Lastly, off the fire, add lemon juice to the cream sauce.

(Serves 4.)

Duck with Sweet Corn

(KACSA KUKORICAVAL)

Rumania-Transylvania

This is a centuries old recipe that is known still among the Hungarian population of the Transylvanian part of Rumania, in the district called Torda. Transylvanian cuisine has a distinct flavor of its own and is much appreciated by Rumanians as well as Hungarians.

1 or 2 slices white bread, soaked in milk	*3 slices bacon, chopped*
	Liver of duck
1 can sweet corn	*1 duck, 4 to 5 pounds*
Salt	*Coarse salt*
Freshly ground black pepper	

Drain bread. In a mixing bowl put the sweet corn and mix with the bread. Add salt, plenty of pepper, and the bacon. Chop liver finely. Add this to the stuffing. Fill the duck with this mixture and sew up the opening carefully. Rub the outside with coarse salt, set on a rack in a baking dish, and roast in a medium (325°) oven for 1 hour or until the meat is tender. Baste regularly with its own fat, if necessary adding a few tablespoons of water to the pan. Carve up the duck and surround with the corn stuffing.
(*Serves 4.*)

Truffled Turkey Crown Prince Rudolf

(TRUTHAHN KRONPRINZ RUDOLF)

Austria

Heir to Emperor Franz Joseph, Crown Prince Rudolf was regarded as the pace-setter among the young aristocrats of the Austro-Hungarian Empire. He loved everything beautiful and enjoyable: women, good food, elegance, and in general what today we call high life and luxury. He kept a famous table in all of his official and unofficial residences. One of his chefs named this dish in his honor.

1 young turkey about 6–8 pounds	1½–2 cups canned bouillon
Salt	2 tablespoons flour
5 slices bacon	Freshly ground black pepper
1 cup mixed, diced raw vegetables (carrots, parsnips, celery)	2 large fresh truffles (or 1 can truffles), finely sliced

Rub with salt a young turkey that is already prepared for the oven. Cover the breast with thin slices of bacon. In a large saucepan arrange a bed of the mixed vegetables. Place the turkey on top, pour on a cup of canned bouillon, cover, and steam very, very slowly until turkey is tender, about 1½ hours. Remove turkey, cut up into serving pieces, and keep warm. Add flour to the vegetable pulp, thin down with the rest of the bouillon, season with pepper, and add the truffles. Cook for 10 minutes or until the sauce is sufficiently thick. (If preferred, you may rub the vegetables through a strainer first before adding the truffles and the thickening.)

Serve turkey with this sauce and garnish with fried new potatoes. (*Serves 4.*)

GAME

Roast Saddle of Hare

(NYULGERINC SUTVE)

Hungary

All cooks know that game, like good beef, must be well hung and never used immediately after killing. On the Continent, game is treated with due reverence. Larding—the process by which you introduce strips of smoked, fatty larding bacon into the flesh of the game—is almost invariably recommended, with the exception of pheasants or small birds like quail and snipe. Those are wrapped in bacon strips.

For larding, there is a special larding needle through the thicker end of which you insert your strip of fat. It can be obtained in all larger hardware shops or department stores.

Saddle and 2 hind legs of a hare	3 tablespoons butter
2–4 ounces larding bacon or 8 slices bacon	2 tablespoons flour
Salt	¾ cup sour cream (or fresh cream)
Freshly ground black pepper	

Under its outer skin the hare has a second skin, hardly more than a film, which must first be removed with a sharp knife. The saddle is then larded with strips of larding bacon 2 inches long and a quarter inch wide (or, should this be too difficult, is wrapped in slices of bacon).

Well grease a baking dish and put in hare. Salt and pepper it. Heat the butter until it boils and pour immediately over the meat. Let it stand for 1 to 2 hours.

Start baking in a slow (250°) oven. After 15 minutes, add a few tablespoons of water to the pan. Keep basting frequently and cook for another hour. Now blend flour with sour cream and pour this over the meat. Increase oven to 350° and finish off roasting until crisp.

Serve garnished with potato croquettes. Also serve *Preiselbeeren*—mountain cranberries from Central Europe, available at specialty food shops.

(*Serves 4 large, 6 small helpings, depending on size of hare.*)

Hare in Marinade

(IEPURE CU MASLINE)

Rumania

1 hare (or large rabbit)	8 peppercorns
1 cup white wine	2 medium-sized onions,
1 cup water	finely sliced
Salt	3 large, fresh tomatoes,
1 bay leaf	sliced
Sprig of thyme	12 pitted black olives

Place the skinned and cleaned hare in an earthenware dish. Boil together wine and water, pour at once over the meat. Season with salt, bay leaf, thyme, and peppercorns. Cover meat with the sliced onions and sliced tomatoes and add the black olives. Let the hare stand, covered, in a cool place (not in the refrigerator) for 24 hours.

Have ready a well-buttered baking dish and put hare into it.

Pour the marinade over it and roast in a 250° oven for 1½ hours, or until tender, basting it frequently.

Carve and serve with its own sauce.

(*Serves 6.*)

Hare in Paprika Sauce

(NYULPAPRIKAS)

Hungary

1 *hare (or large rabbit)*	2 *teaspoons Hungarian*
Salt	*sweet red paprika*
4 *tablespoons bacon fat*	2 *tablespoons flour*
1 *medium-sized onion,*	½ *cup of sour cream*
finely chopped	

Cut up hare into serving portions (legs into 2 parts, the saddle in 4 crosswise). Remove fine filmy skin. Salt well. Heat bacon fat in a large saucepan and fry the onion till golden. Sprinkle with the paprika and add the pieces of meat. Fry them first over strong heat. Reduce heat, cover, and let simmer very gently, adding, if necessary, cold water by the tablespoonful only during the cooking process. When meat is tender, take pieces out and thicken gravy with the flour. Cook for a few minutes, dilute to correct thinness with more cold water. Cook for 10 more minutes, stirring with a spoon.

Put back meat into sauce, reheat. Remove from heat, add the sour cream.

Serve garnished with either boiled and buttered noodles or BREAD DUMPLINGS (HUSKOVE KNEDLIKY).

(*Serves 6.*)

Glazed Hare

(ZAJICOVE RIZKY VE STAVE)

Czechoslovakia

1 cup water	2 carrots, sliced
1 cup dry red wine	2 stalks parsley
Saddle and hind legs of	1 teaspoon sugar
1 hare	3 ounces larding bacon or
Salt	4 slices bacon, chopped
Juice of 1 lemon	2 tablespoons bacon fat
6 peppercorns	2 tablespoons flour
2 bay leaves	3 tablespoons sour cream

Bring the water and red wine to a boil, pour over the hare, which should be placed in an earthenware dish. Add salt, lemon juice, peppercorns, bay leaves, the sliced carrots, parsley, and sugar. Let the hare stand in a cool place, covered, for 24 to 48 hours.

Remove from the marinade, wipe dry, and lard with strips of bacon or cover with chopped bacon. In a baking dish heat the 2 tablespoons of bacon fat and put in the hare. Begin roasting slowly, in a moderate oven (350°), for half an hour. Now pour over the marinade (unstrained) and, basting frequently, cook until meat is tender, about 1 hour. Remove hare and cut into serving pieces. Meanwhile add the flour to the pan and prepare a thick gravy with the pan juices and sufficient water. Rub through a fine wire sieve, reheat this sauce, and lastly, off the fire, add the sour cream.

Serve hare in sauce and garnish with BREAD DUMPLINGS. (Serves 4.)

Hare on the Spit
(DIULJI ZEC NA RAZNJU)

Yugoslavia

Only young hare should be roasted on the spit. But this recipe is excellent if done also with rabbit.

1 hare	2 large tomatoes
Salt	Melted butter
Freshly ground black pepper	Oil
8–10 slices bacon	Black olives, capers, and chopped onions for
2 large red onions	garnish

Remove only the head of the hare, lightly salt and pepper it, and cover entirely with bacon. Tie bacon securely with string.

Thread first a large onion, then a tomato on your spit. Now comes the hare, then again a tomato, and finally another large onion.

Melt the butter and mix it half-and-half with oil. While the spit turns, frequently brush hare with the oil and butter mixture to keep moist and tasty.

When done, garnish with pitted black olives, a small dish of capers, and onions.
(Serves 4.)

Game Pâté

(NYULPASTETOM)

Hungary

Since only the saddle and the top of the hind legs of a hare are generally used for roasting or marinating, the rest of the meat can be utilized for an excellent game *pâté*.

½ pound stewing pork
½ pound calf's or pork liver
Forelegs, giblets, neck, of 1 hare
Salt
2 cups diced, mixed soup vegetables
2 sprigs of parsley
Juice of 1 lemon
4 ounces larding bacon, chopped
Freshly ground black pepper
3–4 tablespoons sour cream
2 tablespoons butter

Cut pork into small cubes and also the liver. Put the hare-parts together with pork and extra liver in a saucepan and cover with cold water. Add salt, the diced soup vegetables, and the parsley, bring to boil. Cover and let simmer gently until all meats are tender.

Take meat off the bone and together with pork and livers mince twice. Put in a mixing bowl, add the lemon juice, the larding bacon, and pepper. Moisten with the sour cream and melted butter. Work to a smooth paste. Well butter a round ovenproof dish, put in the *pâté*, cover top with aluminum foil, and bake in a 300° oven for 1 hour.

This game *pâté* should be served sliced cold.

(*Serves 8.*)

Roast Partridge

(REBHUHN GEBRATEN)

Austria

Roast partridge garnished with a purée of lentils or served over a bed of mushroom-rice is a great delicacy during the hunting season.

Generally, a person with a good healthy appetite can easily consume a whole partridge by himself, especially since only the young birds get roasted. The older ones are stewed in wine. The size of a partridge is about as big as a *poussin*, or very small spring chicken.

1 partridge per person	Lentil *purée as garnish*
Salt	*(given below)*
Black *pepper*	
Slices of fatty bacon or ham	

Clean bird and immerse for a couple of minutes in water that has reached the boiling point. Take out and put into very cold water immediately. After five minutes, drain thoroughly, rub lightly with salt, sprinkle with pepper. Cover all over with thin strips of fatty bacon or ham (or, even better, with strips of gammon—the fat of a cooked ham). Put in a roasting dish and roast in hot (400°) oven, basting frequently, for 45 minutes. Prepare the following purée:

Lentil Purée:

Cook a half pound of lentils for 1½ to 2 hours in water to which salt, peppercorns, and a bay leaf are added. Rub through a sieve, add a little bacon fat, a few drops of lemon juice, and serve hot. (*Serves 1.*)

Partridge with Mushrooms

(REBHUHN MIT CHAMPIGNONS)

Austria

2 large, not so young partridges	3 tablespoons bacon fat
Salt	1 cup Burgundy
Freshly ground black pepper	Sprigs of parsley and thyme
Flour	½ pound fresh mushrooms, sliced

This method is used for the larger partridges. Clean, rub with salt and dust with pepper. Dip into flour. In a large, heavy frying pan heat the fat and fry the flour-coated partridges on all sides, until golden.

Pour on the red wine, add sprigs of parsley and thyme, cover with lid, and gently stew until almost tender. Add now the sliced mushrooms, and continue cooking for another 15 minutes.

Cut partridges lengthwise into halves and serve on top of RISOTTO with the wine-and-mushroom sauce poured over. (Serves 4.)

Snipe in Champagne

(SZALONKA PEZSGOVEL)

Hungary

Snipe, ortolans, and grouse are gourmet delights. What makes the snipe especially prized by the connoisseur is, apart from the delicate, gamy flavor, the creamy insides, which, like a liver paste, are served together with the bird on a slice of toast.

1 snipe per person	2 tablespoons canned
Bacon slices to cover bird	bouillon
Salt	½ cup champagne
Freshly ground black pepper	

Clean the snipe of its feathers only, bring the hind legs forward to rest against the head. The snipe has a long, sharp beak, thread this through the legs. This is the correct way of trussing snipe.

Cover entirely with thin bacon strips. In a heavy, deep frying pan begin to fry snipe, turning it over frequently, until bacon has melted. Carefully salt and pepper, moisten with the concentrated bouillon, or stock, cover with lid, and cook for 25 minutes. Now pour over a half cup of dry champagne and immediately withdraw from the fire.

Remove the insides of the snipe, working very quickly. Discard the giblets but preserve the intestines. Chop them very finely and season with a little salt and black pepper. Moisten with a few drops of champagne and serve as a garnish to the bird, on crisp, hot toast.

(Serves 1.)

Pheasant with Sauerkraut

(KAPOSZTAS FACAN)

Hungary

In prewar Hungary it was not uncommon to bag some thirty to fifty pheasants in one organized shooting. The thirty pheasants were counted for one gun—since the communal bag after a big beat went into the hundreds. Laid side by side, with geometrical precision—hares to one side and pheasants to the other—they formed a magnificent carpet. I have seen photographs of bags where two thousand hares and a thousand pheasants gave testimony to the hunters' skill.

With such abundance of game, it was not surprising that our cooks, getting tired of roasting the pheasants, ventured into methods less orthodox than that: cooking the bird with common sauerkraut. I must say that the result was even more pleasing to our jaded palates.

1 pheasant	8–10 peppercorns
¼ pound larding bacon,	1 bay leaf
or 8–10 slices bacon	1½ pounds fresh or
½ cup white wine	canned sauerkraut
Salt	½ cup beer

Clean pheasant and lard breast and legs with bacon or wrap the whole bird in bacon slices and truss. Place in a deep saucepan, fry first, turning all over until the bacon is rendered. Pour over white wine, add salt, peppercorns, and bay leaf. Cover and gently stew for 1 hour (or until almost tender). Now add the sauerkraut, correct seasoning if necessary, and pour on the beer. Cover and stew for 25 more minutes.

(*Serves 6–8 depending on size of pheasant.*) This recipe is suitable especially when the bird is older and tougher.

Roast Pheasant

(FASAN IM SPECKHEMD)

Austria

This is the orthodox way to prepare pheasant in Austria. Guinea hen, when pheasant is unobtainable, lends itself perfectly to this method of cooking.

To Prepare:

Clean and dress the pheasant, rub with salt and pepper. Cover breast entirely with thin bacon slices and tie up with string.

Use some extra bacon fat for the roasting, which must be like that for chickens, slow and frequently basted with the fat. Pheasant wrapped entirely in bacon can also be done on the spit.

In Austria, the classical garnish is red cabbage (see recipe for DUCKLING WITH RED CABBAGE).

(Serves 6.)

Stewed Pheasant

(BAZANT)

Czechoslovakia

Use this method only for the older and tougher pheasant, which, if roasted, would be too dry.

3 tablespoons bacon fat or lard	Salt
1 pheasant	5–8 peppercorns
1 medium-sized red onion, finely chopped	2 tablespoons flour
2 carrots, diced	1 cup canned bouillon or stock
1 sprig of parsley	3 tablespoons sour cream (or fresh cream)
1 lemon	

Heat bacon fat in a large saucepan. Fry the whole pheasant lightly on all sides. Add the onion, diced carrot, parsley, and half of a lemon cut in slices. Add salt and peppercorns. Moisten with a little lukewarm water, cover and stew on top of the stove until tender, about 1½–2 hours. If necessary, add a little more cold water at a time.

When pheasant is cooked, carve and keep warm. Add the flour to the stewed vegetables, dilute with the canned bouillon or stock, let boil gently for a few minutes and strain. Remove from flame, add the sour cream and the juice of the other half of the lemon. Serve pheasant with this hot sauce.
(Serves 6.)

Wild Duck in Red Wine

(VADKACSA VOROSBORBAN)

Hungary

Around Lake Balaton, the Neusiedler Lake, and in southern Hungary, where the Danube is surrounded by marshland, wild duck and goose are plentiful. However, one should take care of using only young duck and especially young goose, since the older birds remain tough even if treated with the utmost care.

1 wild duck	4–6 peppercorns
½ cup water	1 ounce dried mushrooms
¾ cup dry red wine	4 tablespoons bacon fat
Salt	2 lumps sugar
½ red onion	

Clean off feathers and discard insides of the duck. While still raw, cut up into serving portions. In a deep saucepan put water, ½ cup of the red wine, salt, the red onion, peppercorns, and the dried mushrooms together with the bacon fat. Bring this mixture to boil and put in the duck meat. Cover, reduce heat, and very gently simmer until the meat is tender, about 1¼ hours.

Now caramelize the lump sugar in a separate saucepan and add the rest of the red wine; pour this over the duck and bring to boil only once. Discard onion, serve duck with the wine-flavored sauce.

(Serves 3.)

Young Wild Boar in Sauce

(FRISCHLING NACH FRUHLINGSART)

Austria

There is a restaurant called the White Swan in Vienna. Since restaurants called White Swans are all over Austria, this one distinguishes itself as Gasthof Wegenstein-Weisser Schwan. Here they prepare the wild boar according to a recipe handed down to the proprietor from the court chef to His Royal Highness, Archduke Johann, who was called Herr Zelena. The date: 1832!

The legs of a young wild boar	Sprigs of thyme
2 cups white wine	1 sprig of parsley
1½ cups vinegar	4 cloves
2 cups water	1 stick cinnamon
5 white onions	3 tablespoons bacon fat
2 shallots, finely chopped	3 cloves garlic
Salt	1–2 tablespoons flour
8 peppercorns	Cumberland Sauce (given
3 bay leaves	below)

Remove hard skin (inner skin) from the skinned legs of a young wild boar. Place in a deep, large saucepan and pour on it the wine, vinegar, and water. Add whole white onions, the chopped shallots, salt, peppercorns, bay leaves, thyme, parsley, cloves, and cinnamon. Bring this to the boil, cover, and let it simmer, very, very gently for a couple of hours or until the meat is tender. Strain liquid through a strainer and retain.

In a separate saucepan heat the bacon fat and fry garlic first, then on all sides the cooked meat. Remove, slice, and

keep warm. Add the fat to the flour, stir, and fry for a few
minutes, and now dilute with the cooking liquid strained off
the wild boar. Bring sauce to the correct thickness, by letting it
boil, uncovered, for 15 minutes. Pour over the meat and serve.
Serve with CUMBERLAND SAUCE.
(Serves 8.)

Cumberland Sauce:

4 tablespoons red-currant
    jelly
½ cup port wine
1 teaspoon chopped
    shallots
2 teaspoons chopped
    orange and lemon rind
    mixed

Juice of 1 orange
Juice of ½ lemon
1 teaspoon French mustard
Dash of cayenne pepper

Dissolve the red-currant jelly over fire. Add the port wine,
chopped shallots, the chopped rind of orange and lemon (scald
them in hot water first, then press and cool). Add now the
juice of the orange and the half lemon, the mustard and the
cayenne pepper. Mix very well, and chill. This sauce is always
served cold.

Saddle of Venison

(REHRUCKEN)

Austria

Saddle of venison	1 sprig of parsley
4 ounces larding bacon	1 cup canned bouillon
Salt	3 tablespoons sour cream
Freshly ground black	1 teaspoon French mustard
pepper	Juice of ½ lemon
4 tablespoons butter	BREAD DUMPLINGS or noodles
1 large carrot, diced	as garnish
1 parsnip, diced	Mountain cranberries

Clean saddle of venison, which must be well hung. Cut strips 2 inches long and half an inch wide from the bacon and with a larding needle introduce into the meat. Now rub saddle with salt and dust with plenty of black pepper. In a saucepan heat the butter to a boil and pour immediately over the meat. Let stand for 1 hour, or until butter is hard all over.

Preheat oven to 400° and put in the larded and buttered venison. After 20 minutes, add diced carrot, parsnip, and parsley. Moisten with bouillon. Reduce heat to first 300°, then in 15 minutes to 200°, and very slowly, basting frequently, roast the venison until meat is tender. Pour on the sour cream and let melt.

Take meat out and cut in serving portions. Keep warm. Rub the vegetables and pan gravy through a strainer, reheat. If necessary, thin down with a little more bouillon. Blend in the mustard and, off the fire, add the fresh lemon juice.

Serve meat with this sauce and garnished with BREAD DUMPLINGS or with wide noodles, boiled and tossed in butter. Serve *Preiselbeeren*, mountain cranberries, as a condiment (available at specialty shops). (*Serves 4–6.*)

Meats

THE *WIENER SCHNITZEL* TREE

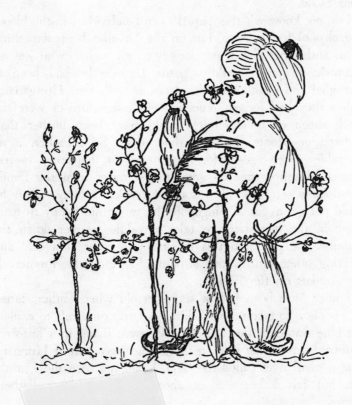

I was brought up on mashed carrots and spinach by a succession of imported governesses from Germany who believed in stern discipline and no salami for breakfast. Contrary to popular belief, goulash was not the staple Hungarian diet; in fact, I remember it figuring on our table only on days when the washerwoman came, and she had to be given something substantial and filling to withstand the drafts in the washroom in the cellar. You become aware of goulash only when you go abroad, preferably in exile, where people expect you to conform to the romantic myth according to which the Danube is blue and all Hungarians have an extra dash of paprika in their blood.

I do not know whether paprika can be absorbed in the blood, like alcohol for instance, but on the Danube I am something of an authority. This I owe largely to my father, who was an eccentric, to put it mildly, partly because he had been to Shanghai and to other exotic places as well. Few Hungarians, unless they had forged somebody else's signature or were the black sheep of their family would have been farther than Abbazia or Monte Carlo in those days. Still, Father, a respectable citizen except for his wanderlust, happened to feel that no distance was too great to get away from the family occasionally. He also liked solitude, which is why, when he could not get as far as Singapore, he was quite happy to roam alone in the mountains or take a paddle steamer down the Danube. He preferred this to sitting in front of a café and greeting other Hungarians strolling by along the Promenade des Anglais on the Riviera.

I must have been five or six years old when Father started on his plans to take me with him on a trip on a raft to explore the blue waters of the Danube. We were living in a fair-sized country town at that time in the northeastern part of Hungary, near a small river called the Sajo. I had not seen the Danube yet, but felt I knew a lot about it already from Father's stories.

We began work on the raft in our vineyard, under the skeptical eyes of my governess, Fräulein Käte. The more she disapproved the greater our joy was as we sawed away on planks or hammered huge nails into the wood that was to become our raft. The wood came from an abandoned hut where once upon a time a reformed gypsy, who worked for us as a guardian, used to live. I remember him well; he always carried a gun, for, as he explained, he needed it to chase away the thieves during the season when the grapes were ripe for the harvest.

"We shall put it on the train," my father said, looking very professional as he spoke with his mouth full of nails. "Then we shall unload it in the Black Forest and start on our trip down the river."

"Herr Doktor," said Fräulein Käte, "I wish you wouldn't put these ideas into the child's head. They will make her only more restless."

"What's wrong with the Black Forest, Fräulein?" Father teased her. "I thought that you came from there yourself."

"I beg your pardon, Herr Doktor," she protested. "I am from Dresden."

"Then it must have been Fräulein Brunhilde," said Father matter-of-factly, referring to Käte's predecessor. "Now that you say it, I remember it was Brunhilde who came from Donauschlingen."

"Is the Black Forest very dark?" I asked with a sudden sense of uneasiness. I disliked the mountains and was afraid of the dark ever since Fräulein Renata, the predecessor of Brunhilde, had locked me up in a dark room for spitting the spinach in her face.

Father realized at once that something was wrong. "Don't you know," he said, "that it is in the Black Forest that the *Wiener schnitzel* tree grows? Never mind that the forest is black, we shall take a torch with us. And we'll find the tree and then you won't be hungry when we start on our trip. You will eat as many *Wiener schnitzels* as you can pick from the tree. And take the rest with us in a knapsack."

My eyes lit up. "With fried potato chips? Are there potato-chip trees too in the Black Forest?"

"Nonsense," said Fräulein Käte quickly, before Father could answer me. "*Wiener schnitzel* doesn't grow on trees. Besides the Black Forest is in Germany and everybody knows that *Wiener schnitzel* comes from Vienna."

"Don't you believe her," said my father, laughing. "How would she know when she's from Dresden herself. What would she know about the Danube or the *Wiener schnitzel?* As a matter of fact," he went on, addressing himself to Fräulein Käte directly, "I doubt that you have ever heard about the Island of the Roses, have you, Fräulein? An island where so many roses are blooming that you think you are in Paradise long before you even sight it from the boat."

"Where is this island?" I asked.

"In Bulgaria," Father answered. "It is an island only for men. They live there and wear turbans on their head just like Aladdin did in the 'Thousand and One Nights.'"

"Can we go and see them?" I asked excitedly.

"Only if I disguise you as a boy. They are like monks and they don't like young ladies to come and disturb them. And I don't blame them. All they do is grow roses all day and pray at night. From the roses they distill an essence which is called *atar.* Once I stayed with them for a whole week," he said nostalgically.

Fräulein Käte made a face, but Father ignored her. "When we leave the island we shall soon approach the delta," he continued. "This is where the Danube splits up in three parts before it enters the Black Sea. There you'll see birds you have never seen before. Egrets and sea gulls and storks. Millions of birds."

"Is the Danube really blue?" I asked changing the subject.

"It isn't!" answered Fräulein Käte. "A blue river is just as much nonsense as a country that calls itself a kingdom and has no king, only an admiral to rule it on horseback." She gave a superior laugh. "The Danube is a dirty, mud-colored river."

"I am sorry to disagree with you, Fräulein," said my father politely. "Ours may be a nonsense-country, but about the Danube you're definitely wrong. It can be blue. It is blue sometimes."

"When?" she asked skeptically.

"When you are in love," said Father simply. "I happened to have seen it myself. I was standing on the Elizabeth Bridge. And though it was winter and the sky was overcast, the Danube nevertheless was a deep, soft blue."

"I have never seen it blue," Fräulein Käte persisted, adjusting the straw boater firmly on her head.

"I am sorry, then you have never been in love, Fräulein," said Father, hitting a rusty nail hard with a hammer. "I am sorry for you, but it can't be helped. Try it once. Who knows? You may agree with me in the end."

BEEF

Beefsteak Nestroy

(BEEFSTEAK NESTROY)

Austria

4 chicken livers	¾ cup strong meat stock or
4 tablespoons butter	canned bouillon
Salt	4 thick slices larding
Freshly ground black	bacon
pepper	4 thick fillet steaks
1 level tablespoon flour	

Clean and coarsely chop the chicken livers. Heat 2 tablespoons of butter in a frying pan and fry livers till golden at quick heat. Add very little salt, a little pepper, and stir in the flour. Continue frying for a few minutes, then pour on the stock and let simmer gently for 5 minutes. Keep warm. Broil bacon till crisp, keep it warm.

Now in a separate frying pan heat the other 2 spoonfuls of butter and fry fillets at strong heat, first one side then the other. Salt and pepper them, serve on a preheated plate and heap a little of the chopped chicken livers on each, decorating each with the bacon.

(Serves 4.)

Whole Fillet of Beef

(BELSZIN EGYBESUTVE)

Hungary

5 ounces larding bacon cut into larding strips	Salt
	Freshly ground black
1 whole piece of fillet, weighing 2 to 2½ pounds	pepper
	¾ cup sour cream
4 tablespoons melted butter	½ cup water

With a larding needle insert the strips of bacon in the meat. Place in a baking dish and pour over it the 4 tablespoons of butter heated to boiling point. Sprinkle with salt and pepper. Let stand for a few hours, the longer the better. Place the baking dish on top of your stove and fry fillet on all sides at brisk heat.

Transfer to a preheated 350° oven, pour over it the sour cream mixed with the water, and roast, basting frequently, for 35 minutes.

Your fillet done this way will be crisp on the outside and pink inside. Pour half of the pan juices over the sliced meat and serve the other half in a sauceboat separately.

(Serves 8.)

Boiled Beef Austrian Style

(BEINFLEISCH ODER TAFELSPITZ)

Austria

This traditional Viennese dish is made from the choice cut of fat boiling beef and served with grated horseradish and soup vegetables as a garnish.

The soup (see recipe for BEEF BROTH) is served clear, either in a cup or in deep soup plates.

2½ pounds boiling beef	3 carrots, sliced lengthwise
(Shin or brisket end of	2 parsnips, sliced
flap)	1 stalk celery
2½ quarts water	½ celery root (if
Salt	obtainable)
8 peppercorns	1 large red onion
2 bay leaves	1 lump sugar

Set the meat to boil in salted water, skim, and let simmer gently for 1 hour. Add peppercorns, bay leaves, vegetables, and the whole onion (with its red outer skin, which gives color to the soup), and sugar. Continue cooking slowly until meat is tender—about another hour and a half.

Take out the meat and slice it. Place it on a preheated platter, surround with the cooked vegetables, and serve freshly grated horseradish separately.

(Serves 6.)

Fillet Steaks Schönbrunn Style

(SCHONBRUNNER RINDFILET)

Austria

1 cup boiled water, cooled	½ onion, sliced
½ cup white wine vinegar	4 large fillet steaks, about
Juice and rind of 1 lemon	1½ inches thick each
2 tablespoons oil	2 tablespoons butter
5 cloves	Salt
2 bay leaves	1 tablespoon flour
8 peppercorns	

Prepare a marinade the following way: Mix the boiled (but already cold) water with the wine vinegar, the juice and rind of a lemon, and the oil. Add cloves, bay leaves, peppercorns, and the sliced onion.

Place fillets 24 hours ahead in this marinade, cover, and keep in a cool place (but not in the refrigerator). Heat butter in a frying pan and fry each steak (drained of the marinade) first on one side then on the other. Salt and remove and keep hot, while blending flour with the strained marinade in the frying pan and letting it boil for 3 minutes. Pour a little of this sauce over each fillet steak. Serve with mashed potatoes and green peas.

(Serves 4.)

Pot Roast Esterházy

(ESTERHAZY ROSTELYOS)

Hungary

This dish bears the name of one of Hungary's most famous families, the Princes Esterházy. The pot roast can be made with equal success from the cheaper cuts of beef, like topside or stewing beef, as well as sirloin steak. The difference is in cooking time only—sirloin steak is minute-fried, whereas topside needs long, slow cooking, always on top of the stove.

2 *pounds flank steak or* *top round or stewing* *beef*
Plain flour
3 *tablespoons bacon fat or* *lard*
1 *small red onion,* *chopped*

2 *teaspoons Hungarian* *sweet red paprika*
Salt
1 *carrot, diced*
2 *sprigs of parsley*
2 *cups stock or canned* *bouillon*
4 *tablespoons sour cream*

Cut beef into thin slices and pound well with a meat hammer. Dredge in flour. Heat the fat in a saucepan, and fry the meat on both sides at brisk heat. Remove and in the same fat fry the onion until golden. Sprinkle with the paprika, replace meat, add salt, the diced carrot, and parsley. Cover with lid, stew very slowly, moistening it occasionally with stock or bouillon. When meat is tender (about 1 hour), put gravy through a strainer, flavor it with the sour cream and serve poured over meat. Garnish with RISOTTO or mashed potatoes. (*Serves 6.*)

Beef with Gherkins

(ZNOJEMSKA PECENE)

Czechoslovakia

Czechoslovakia is famous for its pickled gherkins "à la Znaim." These gherkins are flavored with dill and are excellent as a garnish for roasts, schnitzels, and in summertime, served ice cold directly from the refrigerator, they are delicious and help to clean the palate. Here the beef roll is stuffed with gherkins, thus the name znojemská pečeně.

1 piece of flank steak or top round, weighing about 2 pounds	2 slices bacon, chopped 2 or 3 sour gherkins Salt
3 tablespoons lard or bacon fat	1 cup stock or canned bouillon
1 teaspoon Hungarian sweet red paprika	1 tablespoon flour ½ cup sour cream
½ cup sliced fresh (or canned) mushrooms	

Cut the piece of beef lengthwise into halves, pound each half very well with a meat hammer. Trim into identical rectangular shape. The meat trimmed off is put through a grinder. Heat a tablespoonful of lard or fat, sprinkle with paprika, and lightly fry the ground meat. Mix with the sliced mushrooms, the bacon, and spread this over half of the meat. Lay 2 to 3 sour gherkins in the middle, season with salt, cover with the second half of the meat, and roll up tightly. Tie all around with string.

Heat 2 tablespoons of the fat in a deep saucepan, put in meat, and fry all over till golden. Add half the stock or bouillon, cover with lid, and steam very slowly, for about 1½

hours, or until tender. Remove string, slice, and keep warm. Add flour to the fat in the pan, dilute with rest of stock, and add sour cream. Serve meat with this sauce and garnish with potatoes or BREAD DUMPLINGS.
(*Serves 6.*)

Pot Roast with Piquant Sauce

(SVICKOVA PECENE NA SMETANE)

Czechoslovakia

6 slices bacon	1 bay leaf
1 piece flank steak or top round, weighing about 2 pounds	2 or 3 cups stock or canned bouillon
	1 teaspoon sugar
Salt	Juice of 1 lemon
6 peppercorns	½ cup dry red wine
1 red onion, sliced	½ cup sour cream
1 large carrot, sliced	

Line the bottom of a large saucepan with the bacon. Put the roast on top, add salt, peppercorns, onion, carrot, and bay leaf. Moisten with very little stock or bouillon, cover with lid, and steam on top of the stove for 2 hours, or until meat is tender. Add, when necessary, a little more stock. Slice meat, keep warm. Put gravy through a strainer, flavor with sugar, the juice of a lemon, and the red wine. Bring to a boil once, remove from flame, add the sour cream.

Serve roast with this sauce poured on and garnish with BREAD DUMPLINGS.
(*Serves 6–8.*)

Bulgarian Beef Casserole

(SOFIA GIVETSCH)

Bulgaria

This casserole, called *givetsch*, is known both in Yugoslavia and in Bulgaria. It is a well-known Balkan specialty and very frequently served in summer, when the green pepper and tomato season is on.

2 *pounds stewing beef*	*Salt*
4 *tablespoons oil*	*Freshly ground black*
2 *large onions, sliced*	*pepper*
4 *large green or yellow*	2 *teaspoons Hungarian*
peppers, sliced	*sweet red paprika*
lengthwise	2 *tablespoons chopped*
1 *pound fresh (or canned)*	*parsley*
tomatoes, quartered	*Plain yoghurt to be*
1 *pound potatoes*	*served separately*

Cut beef into cubes and put in a saucepan with the oil. Cover with lid and let fry, very slowly, on top of the stove for 15 minutes. Transfer into an ovenproof casserole, cover with the onion, the peppers, the tomatoes, and the potatoes, cut lengthwise into 4 slices. Season with salt, pepper, and the paprika and sprinkle with parsley. Cover casserole with a tight-fitting lid and place in a 300° oven. Let cook for 15 minutes before reducing oven temperature to very low (250°). Leave casserole for 1½ to 2 hours and, only if necessary, moisten with a little water or stock. Serve yoghurt separately.
(Serves 8.)

Rumanian Beef Hamburgers

(CHIFTELUTA)

Rumania

3 slices milk-soaked white
  bread
1 pound best-quality
  ground beef
Salt
2 cloves garlic, crushed

Black pepper
2 teaspoons chopped
  parsley
1 egg
Oil or bacon fat for frying

Soak the bread in milk, squeeze dry. In a bowl put the
ground meat, add salt, crushed garlic, pepper, and chopped
parsley. Put the bread through a strainer and add to meat,
together with the egg. Work into a smooth paste. With wet
hands shape round balls the size of a golf ball, flatten them to
look like a hamburger, and broil or fry in fat till crisp and
golden on both sides.
(Serves 4.)

Barbecued Ground Beef Sausages

(MITITE)

Rumania

Those who have been to Rumania will always remember those
little barbecued meat sausages, called *mitite*, which are a
national specialty there. You will find them being cooked over
charcoal in the streets or at market-fairs. *Mitite* vendors in

Bucharest line small alleys with their charcoal stoves, and here the whole town comes for a summer-night stroll and a little gourmandizing. *Mitite* can also be served as a cocktail hors d'oeuvre and with it one generally serves sharp, hot peppers.

1 *pound beef, ground*	1 *large onion, minced*
twice	3 *tablespoons cold water*
Salt	2 *tablespoons beef drippings*
Freshly ground black	*or oil*
pepper	*Hot peppers*
2 *teaspoons mixed, crushed*	
thyme, marjoram, and	
bay leaf	

The best cut for ground beef should come from the neck of the beef. Put the meat in a mixing bowl, add salt, pepper, the herbs, and the minced onion, work into a very smooth paste with the aid of the water. This should be done a day ahead. Now wrap the meat paste in a damp cloth, place in refrigerator overnight.

Next day, rework paste and add the beef fat, preferably, or oil. Shape with wet hands 2-inch-long and very thin sausages and grill them over a charcoal fire. Serve hot or cold, with sharp, hot peppers separately.

(*Serves 12 as an hors d'oeuvre.*)

Yugoslav Broiled Beef Sausages

(CEVAPCICI)
Yugoslavia

Very similar to the Rumanian *mitite* only it is sometimes made
with half beef, half veal. The only other difference is that in
Yugoslavia these little sausages are invariably served with a
small plate of chopped raw onion for each person and a fresh
tomato salad.

Austrian Hamburgers

(FASCHIERTES)

These hamburgers are made similar to the Rumanian *chif-
teluta,* only in Austria they prefer to use half beef, half veal
(or even a third of beef, a third of veal, and a third of pork)
for the meat. The mince is stretched with the addition of milk-
soaked bread. *Faschiertes* are always served in round hamburger
form, and often, instead of being garnished with potatoes, rice,
etc., they are served on top of a dish of puréed spinach or other
vegetables. In this case they are called an *Auflag,* or, literally
translated, "on top."

Transylvanian "Wooden Platter"

(ERDELYI FATANYEROS)

Rumania, Hungary

This very attractive mixed grill is served on a large wooden platter (you can ask for it in both Hungarian as well as Rumanian restaurants), which gives it its name: *Fatányéros.*

Serve per person:

> 1 *fillet or sirloin steak, broiled*
> 1 *lamb chop, broiled*
> 1 *pork chop, broiled*
> (*sausages, liver, or kidney, broiled, is sometimes served with the above*)

Garnish with:

> Pan-fried potatoes   Sour gherkins
> Boiled rice   Spring onions
> Beet salad (pickled)

Allow 1 wooden platter for 2 persons. Heap the broiled cuts in the middle and arrange the various garnishes decoratively around them.

Real Hungarian Goulash

(GULYAS LEVES)

Hungary

See GOULASH SOUP.

Austrian Goulash

(GOULASH)

Austria

Austrian goulash differs only from the Hungarian in that more onions are used (sometimes half and half with the beef) and also, in addition to the sweet red paprika, in Austria they add *kümmel* or caraway seed.

Yugoslav Goulash

(GULAS)

Yugoslavia

The Yugoslav goulash is prepared as the Hungarian, with the addition of green peppers, fresh tomatoes, and garlic.

Rumanian Goulash

(TOCANA)

Rumania

In Rumanian goulash is called *tocana* and can be made with beef, mutton, or pork. Here also onion is used in great quantity, and is not fried first, as in Hungarian goulash, but is added later, chopped.

Bulgarian Goulash
(GOULASH)
Bulgaria

Made exactly like the Yugoslav version.

VEAL

Breaded Veal Cutlets

(WIENER SCHNITZEL)

Austria

Though *Wiener schnitzel* is a dish that is known all over the world, a real good *schnitzel* is still hard to find outside Austria or in restaurants other than Austrian-owned. There are little secrets that belong to this dish: the cut of veal firstly, which must be off the leg (the rump); the way it is fried, which is best described as semideep-frying; and lastly that it should be made to order, since standing and reheating make the *Wiener schnitzel* soggy.

4 slices of leg of veal,	*Salt*
about ¾ pound	*Finely sifted breadcrumbs*
Flour	*1 part butter and 1 part*
1 egg	*oil for semideep-frying*

Clean veal slices and remove all gristle and skin. Flatten to less than a quarter of an inch thickness with a meat hammer. Do not wash. Coat with plain flour all over. Dip into the beaten egg, which is seasoned with salt. Roll into finely sifted (preferably homemade) fresh breadcrumbs.

In a heavy frying pan heat 1 part oil and 1 part butter. To fry 4 large *schnitzeln,* you need about 1 cup of the fat. The fat must be boiling hot when the meat is put in. Fry first on 1 side at brisk heat until golden. Turn over and fry the other side.

Never turn over the second time, since this would make the crumbs stick to the pan.

Drain on absorbent paper—the *schnitzel*, must be crisp and free of all extra grease.

Garnish with mashed potatoes, slices of lemon, and fresh parsley.

(*Serves 4.*)

Veal Cutlets

(NATURSCHNITZEL)

Austria

1 *pound leg of veal*	*Butter for frying*
Flour	½ *cup water*
Salt	*Juice of* ½ *lemon*
Freshly ground black	
pepper	

Cut leg of veal lengthwise into half-inch-thick slices. Clean off all gristle and lightly flatten with a meat hammer. Coat all over with flour seasoned with salt and pepper.

In a heavy skillet heat the butter and when hot brown meat first on 1 side, then on the other. Pour on the water, cover with a lid, reduce heat, and let cook for 10 minutes. Lastly squeeze in the lemon juice—there should be no more than 1 spoonful of pan juice left, which is sufficient to moisten the cutlets.

Serve with mashed potatoes and decorate with fresh parsley. (*Serves 4.*)

Veal Steaks with Mushrooms

(GOMBAS BORJUSZELET)

Hungary

1 *pound leg of veal, cut into steaks*	1 *teaspoon Hungarian sweet red paprika*
2 *tablespoons lard, bacon fat, or butter*	1 *cup sliced mushrooms (fresh or canned)*
Salt	1 *tablespoon flour*
1 *cup canned bouillon or stock*	½ *cup water*
	½ *cup sour cream*

Cut veal into small, inch-thick steaks. (You may use, if obtainable, the fillet of veal.)

In a heavy frying pan heat the fat and brown the steaks on each side at strong heat. Season with salt, pour on the canned bouillon or stock, sprinkle with the paprika. Reduce heat and cover pan with a lid. Let cutlets cook for 5 minutes. Add the mushrooms, cook for 10 more minutes.

Remove meat and keep warm. Blend in flour with the fat and the mushrooms, stir and fry for a few minutes. Moisten with half a cup of cold water, let sauce thicken sufficiently. Put back meat, reheat, remove from flame, and add the sour cream.

Serve with mashed potatoes, rice, or buttered noodles. (*Serves 4.*)

Veal Paprika

(BORJUPORKOLT)

Hungary

Some people tend to mistake veal paprika for veal goulash. The fact is that veal is never made with a lot of gravy, like a goulash, nor are potatoes cooked with it. The gravy must be scant, the reddish-gold color of the Hungarian paprika, and with the real *pörkölt* one adds no sour cream in the end. If sour cream is added, the dish is called *borju paprikás*.

1½ pounds stewing veal (knuckle or flap)	1 level tablespoon Hungarian sweet red
1 small red onion, finely chopped	paprika
	Salt
3 tablespoons lard or bacon fat	2 tablespoons flour
	1 cup bouillon or stock

Cut veal into small cubes and chop the onion. In a saucepan heat the lard or bacon fat, fry the onion until golden. Sprinkle with the paprika and add the meat. Fry at brisk heat, stirring all the time, until meat changes color and is lightly fried.

Season with salt, cover with lid and reduce heat. Let the meat stew in its own juices for 35 minutes. (If veal is slightly old, stew until tender—if necessary moistening it with a spoonful of cold water occasionally.)

Move meat to one side and blend in the flour, increase heat, fry for a few minutes. Dilute with the bouillon or stock, reduce heat, and let gravy thicken, boiling it without a lid for another 6 to 10 minutes. Serve garnished with EGG DUMPLINGS. (*Serves 4.*)

Veal Olives or Rolls

(GEBRATENES KALBSVOGERL MIT SCHINKENREIS)

Austria

1 pound leg of veal	Freshly ground black
RISOTTO for 4–6 persons	pepper
½ cup ground or finely chopped ham	1 teaspoon chopped parsley
Flour	1½ cups canned bouillon
4 tablespoons butter	or stock
Salt	

Cut leg of veal into quarter-inch slices. Remove all gristle and pound meat with a meat hammer.

Prepare the RISOTTO (rice dry-fried in butter and then boiled). Mix with the finely chopped ham. Spread this mixture over each thin slice of veal, roll up, and tie securely with thread, similar to small parcels. Roll lightly in flour.

In a frying pan heat the butter and fry veal rolls until golden on all sides. Add salt, pepper, and parsley, moisten with half a cup of bouillon or stock. Put on lid, reduce heat, and cook slowly for 15 minutes. Remove rolls and keep warm. Add 2 tablespoons flour to the pan, stir, and fry for a few minutes. Dilute with the rest of the bouillon, let simmer uncovered till gravy thickens. Put back the meat, reheat, and serve. (*Serves 4–6.*)

Veal Stew with Caraway Seeds

(TELECI GULAS NA KMINA)

Czechoslovakia

1½ *pounds stewing veal* (*knuckle or flap*)	1 *carrot, diced*
3 *tablespoons butter or bacon fat*	1 *stalk celery, diced*
Salt	1½ *cups canned bouillon or stock*
Freshly ground black pepper	2 *tablespoons flour*
2 *teaspoons caraway seeds*	2 *teaspoons chopped parsley*

Cut veal into small cubes. In a saucepan heat the butter and fry meat until golden. Season with salt, pepper, and add the caraway seeds. Cover with lid, reduce heat, and let cook slowly, without any liquid added, for 10 minutes. Now add the diced carrot and celery, moisten with half a cup of bouillon or stock, replace lid, and cook slowly until meat is tender.

Blend in flour, add parsley, and fry for a few minutes. Dilute with the rest of the bouillon, cook uncovered for a few more minutes.

Serve with boiled or mashed potatoes or EGG DUMPLINGS. (*Serves 4.*)

Calf's Brains in Breadcrumbs

(TELECI MOZECEK VE STRONHANCE)

Czechoslovakia

1 pound calf's brains	2 tablespoons butter
Salt	2 tablespoons oil
Flour	1 teaspoon chopped
1 to 2 eggs	parsley
Finely sifted breadcrumbs	1 lemon, sliced

Clean the brains thoroughly under running cold water. Put in a saucepan and barely cover with salted water. Cover and steam for 10 minutes. Drain and clean again if necessary.

Cut each set of brains in half, roll in flour, and dip into beaten egg. Coat all over with breadcrumbs.

Heat butter and oil in a frying pan, fry brains until golden all over. Sprinkle the parsley in the butter and fry for 1 minute. Pour butter over brains and serve, decorated with lemon slices. Garnish with mashed potatoes.

Brains prepared in this way could also be served as a first course with TARTARE SAUCE.

(Serves 4–6.)

Leg of Veal with Rice Stuffing

(TELETINA PUNJENA SA PIRINZOM)

Yugoslavia

1 leg of veal	1 carrot, diced
1 tablespoon butter	1 stalk celery, diced
½ cup sliced mushrooms	1 cup canned bouillon or
1½ cups cooked rice	stock
½ cup peas (fresh or	2 cups peeled, chopped
frozen)	tomatoes (fresh or
Salt	canned)
Freshly ground black	1 tablespoon flour
pepper	
4 tablespoons bacon fat or	
lard	

Make a deep incision in the leg of veal and fill this "pocket" as follows:

In a tablespoon of butter cook the mushrooms for 5 minutes. Add them to the separately boiled rice, together with the peas. Add salt and pepper, stuff inside veal, and carefully sew up the opening. In a large saucepan heat the bacon fat or lard, brown the veal all over at brisk heat.

Add the carrots, celery, if necessary a little more salt and pepper, and moisten with half the stock. Cover with lid, reduce heat, and cook very slowly for half an hour. Now add the tomatoes, replace lid, and continue cooking until meat is tender. (If necessary, moisten occasionally with a spoonful or two of cold water.)

When meat is cooked, remove from pan, add flour to the

vegetables, fry for a few minutes, then dilute with the remaining bouillon in order to obtain a thick gravy.

Slice meat, garnish with the rice stuffing, pour gravy on it, and serve hot.
(Serves 8.)

Roast Breast of Veal

(PUNJENA TELENTINA)

Yugoslavia

3 *slices white bread, soaked in milk*	1 *egg*
Salt	2 *teaspoons chopped parsley*
Freshly ground black pepper	2 *pounds breast of veal*
4 *ounces chopped bacon slices*	4 *cloves garlic*
	4 *tablespoons lard or bacon fat*

In a mixing bowl put in the bread first soaked in milk, then drained thoroughly. Add salt, pepper, chopped bacon, egg, and parsley. Beat with an electric beater until a smooth mixture is obtained.

Cut a large pocket in the veal by lifting up the skin and stuffing with the above mixture. (If you prefer, spread the mixture on top of the flattened meat, then roll it up.) Sew up opening carefully, stud the meat with slivers of garlic.

Heat lard or bacon to boiling point, pour over the meat, and roast in a 250° oven, basting it frequently, for 1½ hours.
(Serves 6.)

Veal or Lamb Sausages

(KEBABCE BULGARIAN STYLE)

Bulgaria

I prefer to make these small hamburger sausages with minced veal. In Bulgaria they are made with either veal or lamb. This dish you will find under different names all through the Near and Middle East.

1 pound veal, ground twice	1 teaspoon red Hungarian hot paprika
1 onion, minced	1 egg
Salt	Flour
Freshly ground black pepper	

In a mixing bowl put the meat, onion, and seasoning of salt, pepper, and paprika. Blend this mixture together with an egg and let rest for 1 hour in a cool place. Wet your hands or dust them with flour. Take small portions of the meat (about a tablespoonful), shape into round balls, then roll into little sausages 2 inches long.

These *kebabce* are best if barbecued or cooked over charcoal heat, but they can be fried also in oil in a heavy iron skillet. They are excellent hot as a main course, or cold as a cocktail hors d'oeuvre.

(*Serves 4 as a main course.*)

Bulgarian Veal Stew

(POPSKA JACHNIA)

Bulgaria

1 pound small whole white onions	Freshly ground black pepper
2 pounds stewing veal	1 teaspoon Hungarian sweet red paprika
3 tablespoons lard or bacon fat	2 cloves garlic, crushed
Salt	1 cup white wine

Remove only the outer skin of the onions. Cut the meat into small cubes. In a saucepan heat the fat and lightly fry the onions, but do not brown them. Add the meat, season with salt, pepper, paprika, and the crushed garlic. Cover with a lid, reduce heat, and stew first without adding any liquid. After 20 minutes pour on the wine, continue stewing till meat is tender.

This recipe can be made with beef, too.

With this dish a bowl of yoghurt is always served separately. (Serves 4–6.)

Transylvanian Veal Stew

(TOCANA)

Rumania

2 *pounds stewing veal*	*Salt*
6 *large red onions*	½ *cup water or canned*
3 *tablespoons bacon fat*	*bouillon*
or lard	

Cut stewing veal into cubes, finely slice (do not chop) the onions. In a saucepan heat the fat, put in the meat, season with salt, and cover with the lid. Reduce heat, let stew, without adding any liquid, for 20 minutes. You must take care with this stew that the meat should not brown, but should steam in its own juices. Now take the finely sliced onion and after moistening the meat with no more than half a cup of water or canned bouillon, add the onions. Cover with lid again, slowly stew till all the water is absorbed and the meat and onions are cooked and dry of gravy. Serve with boiled potatoes.
(*Serves* 8.)

Austrian Veal Stew

(EINGEMACHTES KALBFLEISCH)

Austria

This veal stew should always contain as its base an assortment of root vegetables, such as carrots, parsnips, and celery root. Then, according to the fresh vegetables that come with each season, you may vary the stew, by adding cauliflower in winter, in early spring the first green peas or the tender kohlrabi. The main characteristic of the Austrian stew, or *Eingemachtes*, is that it should have the consistency of a thick soup rather than a stew—that is, you must not boil off all pan juices but keep the gravy thin.

1½ pounds stewing veal	3 tablespoons butter
2 carrots, diced	Salt
1 parsnip, diced	Freshly ground black
1 stalk celery, diced (or	pepper
½ celery root if	2 tablespoons flour
obtainable)	2 teaspoons chopped
1 cup peas	parsley
1 small cauliflower	2 cups stock or canned
(optional)	bouillon

Cut meat into small cubes, dice carrots, parsnip, celery or celery root, shell peas, and break up cauliflower into flowerets. In a large saucepan heat the butter, fry the meat till lightly golden on all sides. Add seasoning of salt and pepper, cover with lid, reduce heat, and steam for 15 to 25 minutes. Add the vegetables, moisten, if necessary, with a little bouillon or water (without, however, letting it acquire a boiled rather than a steamed flavor). Continue cooking until meat is tender—about another half hour.

Boil off all surplus liquid, then sprinkle with the flour and the chopped parsley, fry, stirring for a few minutes, then dilute with the stock or bouillon. Let it boil for 5 minutes more, uncovered, till gravy slightly thickens. Serve with boiled or mashed potatoes. (*Serves 6.*)

Breaded Veal Knuckles

(RANTOTT BORJULAB)

Hungary

2 veal knuckles	Sprig of parsley
3 cups water	Flour
Salt	1 egg
Pepper	Finely sifted breadcrumbs
1 carrot	4 tablespoons bacon fat
1 stalk celery, diced	

Leave knuckles whole and put in a saucepan, cover with 3 cups of cold water. Bring to boil, skim, add salt and pepper, the carrot, sliced in half, celery, and parsley. Cover with lid, cook slowly till meat is tender, about 1 hour. Drain (the liquid makes an excellent stock and should not be discarded) and dry thoroughly.

Take meat off the bone, cutting it off lengthwise into 2 long slices. Dip each piece of meat in flour, then into beaten egg seasoned with salt and pepper, and coat all over with breadcrumbs.

Heat fat in a frying pan and fry the crumbed meat until golden. Serve with either a TARTARE SAUCE or with cold potato salad.

(Serves 4.)

Calf's Liver Paprika

(PORKOLT BORJUMAJ)

Hungary

1 *pound calf's liver*	1 *teaspoon Hungarian*
2 *tablespoons bacon fat*	*sweet red paprika*
1 *small red onion,*	*Salt*
chopped	

Cut liver into half-inch-thick slices and each slice into thin, ribbon-like strips. Cut strips again about one and a half inches long. Do not wash or salt, since this is what toughens liver.

Heat the fat in a frying pan and fry the chopped onion until golden. Sprinkle with the paprika, increase heat, put in the small pieces of liver, and fry, stirring all the time, until liver changes color, about 3 minutes. Serve at once and salt only at the table.

Garnish with EGG DUMPLINGS.

(*Serves 4.*)

Calf's Brains with Kidneys

(VESE VELOVEL)

Hungary

½ pound calf's kidneys
½ pound calf's brains
  (2 sets)
2 tablespoons bacon fat
1 small red onion, finely
  chopped
1 teaspoon Hungarian
  sweet red paprika

½ cup canned bouillon or
  stock
Salt
Freshly ground black
  pepper

Soak the kidneys in cold water for half an hour. Drain and slice thinly. Clean the brains under running cold water and chop while still raw.

In a frying pan heat the fat and fry the onion till golden. Sprinkle with the paprika, put in the kidneys—do not season—and cover with lid. Let steam (without adding any water) for 5 minutes. Remove lid, boil off any excess liquid and add the chopped brains. Stir as you would scrambled eggs for a few minutes, until brains have cooked. Immediately pour the canned bouillon or stock over it, bring to boil, season with salt and freshly ground black pepper, and serve at once, without letting it stand and get tough.

(Serves 4.)

PORK

Styrian Roast Pork

(STEIERISCHER SCHWEINSBRATEN)

Austria

This is the way roast pork is made in Lower Austria, or Styria, through which the Danube passes. The recipe comes from Melk.

1 piece roasting pork (3–4 pounds)	1 teaspoon marjoram
Salt	2 cups stock or canned bouillon
French mustard	4 small white onions, peeled
Freshly ground black pepper	1 rounded tablespoon flour

Take the piece of roasting pork—the cut preferred is the part off which the chops are cut—and rub with salt. Now spread all over with mustard, season with pepper and marjoram, and place in a warm (350°) oven without any additional fat. Roast for 20 minutes, pour on a cup of stock, reduce heat to 250°, and add the onions. Continue roasting slowly, basting frequently, until meat is tender, about 1½ hours. Rub drippings through a sieve, thicken with flour and dilute with more stock or bouillon. Serve with boiled potatoes or BREAD DUMPLINGS.

(Serves 4 according to size of roast.)

Boiled Pork

(GEKOCHTES SCHWEINSFLEISCH)

Austria

The real Austrian specialty is boiled pork, but in Austria the pork is first smoked, like ham. If you cannot obtain the smoked pork chops from an Austrian butcher, you may prepare the following recipe, which is also very much liked in Austria.

2 pounds shoulder-of-pork in one piece (with bones)	6 peppercorns Salt 1 bay leaf
4 teaspoons caraway seeds	2 cloves garlic

Leave pork in 1 piece and do not remove bones. Put in a large saucepan, cover with cold water. Add caraway seeds, peppercorns, and salt, together with bay leaf and whole cloves of garlic. Bring to boil, skim, cover with lid and very gently simmer for 1½ to 2 hours or until meat is tender.

Serve on top of cooked sauerkraut with boiled potatoes. (Serves 4.)

Suckling Pig with Sweet Corn
(PURCEL DE LAPTE)
Rumania

This is a favorite dish in Rumania, where suckling pig is greatly appreciated for its tender meat and delicate flavor.

4 slices white bread, soaked in milk	2 eggs
	4 cups sweet corn
Salt	1 suckling pig
Freshly ground black pepper	1–2 teaspoons sage
	4 tablespoons bacon fat

Soak bread in milk, drain, and rub through a sieve. Add salt, pepper, eggs and sweet corn, mix well for stuffing.

The pig must be thoroughly cleaned inside, but otherwise left whole. Fill cavity with the mixture, sew up. Rub with salt, pepper, sage, and brush the skin all over with bacon fat. Place in a baking dish and add a cup of water to the pan.

Start baking in a hot (400°) oven. After half an hour reduce heat to 350° and 15 minutes later to 300°. Roasting time should be 1½ to 2 hours, depending on size. Lastly, to crispen the skin, increase oven heat to maximum and finish off the roasting process. Serve quickly, while still very hot, and garnish with the corn stuffing, raw red cabbage salad, and boiled potatoes.
(Serves 6–8.)

Pork Chops in Breadcrumbs

(COTLETE PRAJITE)

Rumania

For this dish one must use only very young and not fatty pork. Fresh cucumber salad or pickled sour gherkins are essential garnishes.

8 *young pork chops*	2 *eggs*
Salt	*Fresh breadcrumbs*
Freshly ground black	*Bacon fat or lard for*
pepper	*semideep-frying*
Flour	

Use tender, young pork chops and have them cut very thin. Take a meat hammer and pound meat well on both sides. Rub with salt, dust with pepper, and coat all over with flour. Beat the eggs as if for an omelet, dip each chop into the egg and lastly roll in breadcrumbs.

Heat bacon fat and fry the chops in a frying pan, first on one side until golden brown, then on the other side. Never turn twice to the same side, to prevent crumbs from sticking to the pan. Serve with mashed potatoes, rice, and cucumber salad or sour gherkins with it.

(*Serves 4.*)

Stuffed Grape Leaves

(SARMI)

Bulgaria

You will find this dish under different names throughout the Near East. It is the most delicate and delicious of all Eastern specialties. I have slightly modified it by using minced pork rather than the beef for the stuffing of the leaves.

30–40 *young grape leaves*	½ *cup warm water*
1 *pound pork, ground*	½ *cup uncooked rice*
twice	*Plain yoghurt*
Salt	
Freshly ground black	
pepper	

Remove stems from the young grape leaves and put in a saucepan with very little water. Bring to a boil and turn off immediately. This process makes the leaves pliable. Drain but do not discard water. In a mixing bowl make a smooth paste from the ground pork to which you add salt and pepper, half a cup of warm water, and the rice.

Lay the leaves flat, put in the middle of each a rounded teaspoonful of the filling. Wrap up like a small parcel. Butter a baking dish well, arrange the packages side by side, lightly salt them, and pour over them the water drained off the leaves. Place in a 300° oven and cook for 50 minutes to an hour.

Serve plain yoghurt separately.

This dish is delicious cold and can even be served as a cocktail hors d'oeuvre.

(*Serves 6–8.*)

Pork in Casserole

(BOSANSKI LONAC)

Yugoslavia

This is a Bosnian specialty that makes an excellent one-course meal.

1½ pounds boned leg of
  pork
2 pounds potatoes
5 tablespoons bacon fat or
  lard
Salt
2 teaspoons Hungarian
  sweet red paprika

1½ cups sour cream
4 to 6 large red onions,
  finely sliced
4 large green peppers,
  seeded and finely sliced

Cut the leg of pork into very thin slices and each slice in half. Peel potatoes and slice equally thinly. Take a large earthenware casserole that could go directly to the table and has a tight-fitting lid, grease the bottom and sides well with bacon fat or lard.

Make a layer of the potatoes. Add salt, sprinkle with a little of the paprika, and spread with a thin coating of the sour cream. Scatter with sliced onions and a few slices of green peppers. Cover with the thin slices of meat. Salt the meat again carefully. Grease with fat. Now cover with potatoes again and repeat as above until all the ingredients are used up. Top layer is always potatoes, moistened with sour cream.

Put lid on casserole and put in a 350° oven to start, after 10 minutes reduce to 300°, and 15 minutes later to 250°. Let casserole cook for 2 hours. Serve directly from casserole. (Serves 8.)

Stuffed Sauerkraut

(SARMA)

Yugoslavia

This dish is also made in Hungary, where it is called *töltött káposzta*. You may find it on Austrian menus under the name of *Gefüllte Krautwickerln*. The pickled cabbage leaves are filled with a meat-and-rice mixture and are cooked with finely shredded sauerkraut. Since it is almost impossible to find the large pickled cabbage leaves anywhere outside the Danube countries, I always use fresh green cabbage leaves for the stuffing.

8 *large green cabbage leaves*
2 *pounds fresh or canned sauerkraut*
¾ *pound ground pork*
½ *pound ground beef*
¾ *cup uncooked rice*
Salt
Pepper

2 *cloves garlic, crushed*
½ *cup warm water*
4 *tablespoons bacon fat*
2 *teaspoons Hungarian sweet red paprika*
1 *large red onion, chopped*
Water or stock
5 *tablespoons sour cream*

Soften cabbage leaves in boiling water. Drain and keep for 24 hours with the sauerkraut in an earthenware bowl.

Make a filling with the pork, beef, rice, seasoned with salt, pepper, and garlic. Work into a smooth paste with the lukewarm water.

Put 2 tablespoons of the filling in the middle of each "tenderized" leaf, roll up, tie with string like a neat parcel. Drain the sauerkraut.

In a large saucepan heat the fat, sprinkle with the paprika, and fry the chopped onion lightly. Put in the sauerkraut and on top of the sauerkraut the filled leaves. Correct seasoning. Pour on a cup of water or stock, bring to a boil, cover with lid, and simmer at reduced heat for half an hour. Now add another cup of water and cook slowly. The slower this dish cooks the more it retains its flavor. Cooking time should be 1½ to 2 hours and, if necessary, a little more water or stock should be added as you go along. Lastly, just before serving, pour the sour cream over it.

(*Serves 6.*)

Roast Pork with Dumplings

(VEPROVA PECENE S KNEDLIKY)

Czechoslovakia

4–6 *pounds loin of pork*	1 *cup water*
Salt	1 *cup stock or water*
3 *teaspoons caraway seeds*	2 *tablespoons flour*
1 *teaspoon marjoram*	

Score fat with a sharp knife, rub with coarse salt, sprinkle with caraway seeds and marjoram. Put a cup of water in your roasting pan (pork never needs fat for roasting, only a little water in the pan). Put in pork and roast very slowly, in a slow (250°) oven until meat is tender—about 2½–3 hours. Baste frequently to obtain a crisp, crackling fat on top.

Thicken pan gravy with flour, dilute with stock or water. Slice pork and pour the gravy over it. Garnish with BREAD DUMPLINGS.

(*Serves 6–8.*)

Stuffed Green Peppers in Tomato Sauce

(TOLTOTT PAPRIKA)

Hungary

12 medium-sized green peppers	1½ cups uncooked rice
¾ pound ground pork	½ cup water
½ pound ground beef	3 tablespoons bacon fat
Salt	2 tablespoons flour
Freshly ground black pepper	1 pound canned tomatoes
1 clove garlic, crushed	1½ cups water or canned bouillon
	1 tablespoon tomato paste

Cut top off each pepper and carefully remove seeds. Wash and dry. In a mixing bowl put in the pork and beef, add salt, pepper, and crushed garlic, together with the uncooked rice. Work to a paste with the water and fill each green pepper three-quarters full with this mixture. (Never fill the peppers, since the rice swells while cooking.)

In a large saucepan melt the fat and fry the flour for a few minutes. Add the canned tomatoes, which you have rubbed through a sieve, and also the water or canned bouillon. Blend in the tomato paste, season with salt. In this very thin tomato sauce put in the stuffed peppers, bring carefully to a boil, cover with lid, reduce heat and cook, very, very slowly, for 1 hour. If preferred, the peppers can be cooked in the oven, where they must cook even slower for about 2 hours. (Serves 6.)

Pork Fillets with Piquant Sauce

(SCHWEINSLUNGENBRATEN)

Austria

2 1-pound fillets of pork	1 cup canned bouillon or
Salt	water
2 tablespoons bacon fat	1 tablespoon flour
Black pepper	2 teaspoons chopped
1 large carrot, grated	capers
½ small red onion, minced	4 tablespoons sour cream
1 bay leaf	Juice of ½ lemon

Take the whole fillets of pork and rub with salt. In a large skillet heat the fat and brown meat on all sides. Add the pepper, grated carrot, minced onion, and bay leaf. Moisten with a little bouillon or water. Put lid on and let simmer very gently for 45 minutes.

Remove fillets and cut into inch-thick slices. Blend flour in with the vegetable pulp in the skillet, fry for a few minutes, then dilute with the bouillon. Replace meat in this sauce, heat thoroughly. Lastly add the chopped capers, the sour cream, and the lemon juice, but do not boil again. Serve with mashed potatoes or wild rice.

(Serves 4.)

Pork Goulash and Sauerkraut

(SZEKELYGULYAS)

Hungary

2 pounds fresh or canned
sauerkraut

3 tablespoons bacon fat

1 small red onion, finely
chopped

2 teaspoons Hungarian
sweet red paprika

1½ pounds stewing pork

Salt

1 tablespoon flour

¾ cup sour cream

If fresh sauerkraut is used, wash in several waters, drain, and steam in a saucepan with 3 tablespoons bacon fat and 3 cups water for 45 minutes. If canned sauerkraut (or already cooked) is used, heat only and lightly fry for a few minutes in bacon fat. Prepare a Hungarian pork stew by frying the chopped onion in a tablespoonful of fat until golden. Sprinkle with paprika, put in the meat, cut into small cubes, fry for a few minutes till meat changes color. Add salt, cover with lid, and stew at very low heat until tender, adding, only if necessary, a spoonful of water occasionally.

Mix this pork stew with the cooked sauerkraut. Blend flour with sour cream, pour over stew, and let cook, uncovered, for 5 more minutes.

(Serves 8.)

Pork and Sauerkraut Casserole

(KOLOZSVARI RAKOTTKAPOSZTA)

Hungary-Transylvania

This is one of my favorite dishes to serve for a winter supper. Among the ingredients it is only the paprika sausage that might be difficult to obtain. Should you be unable to find it in a specialty shop where Hungarian sausages are sold, substitute dry Polish sausage or the Spanish pork sausage called *churro*.

1 *pound stewing pork*	4 *hard-cooked eggs, sliced*
1 *onion*	1½ *pounds canned*
2 *teaspoons Hungarian*	*sauerkraut*
sweet red paprika	2 *cups boiled rice*
4 *tablespoons bacon fat*	½ *cup sour cream*
½ *pound dry Hungarian*	
paprika sausage	

Prepare first a pork goulash from the stewing pork, chopped onion, paprika, and 1 tablespoon of bacon fat. (See recipe for PORK GOULASH AND SAUERKRAUT.)

Grease a large earthenware casserole with bacon fat. Thinly slice sausage and slice eggs. Make a layer first with the cooked sauerkraut, then with rice, then pork goulash, then again sauerkraut. Now comes another layer of dried paprika sausage, sliced eggs. Again sauerkraut, rice, pork goulash. Continue till all ingredients are used up. The top layer is sauerkraut. Spread thickly with sour cream and bake in a moderate (350°) oven for half an hour to 1 hour.

(*Serves 6–8.*)

Special Pork Chops "Blue Danube"

(SERTESKARAJ "KEK DUNA" MODRA)

Hungary

This is one of the most original recipes for pork chops. It was given to me by the prewar chef of the famous Budapest restaurant called Blue Danube, or Kék Duna.

1 tablespoon lard or bacon fat	Pepper
½ red onion, minced	2 fresh tomatoes, quartered
4 large pork chops, weighing ½ pound each	1 large green pepper
	½ pound dry paprika sausage
1 teaspoon Hungarian sweet red paprika	2 slices bacon, chopped
Salt	1 cup sour cream

In a large, heavy skillet heat the lard or bacon fat and fry the onion till golden. Sprinkle the chops with paprika and fry on both sides until golden. Add salt, pepper, and scatter the tomatoes on top, along with the sliced green pepper, the sausage, cut into thin slices, and the chopped bacon. Cover with lid, reduce heat, and let cook very slowly for 30 minutes. Pour in the sour cream, heat to boiling point, and serve at once with a garnish of RISOTTO or EGG DUMPLINGS. (Serves 4.)

LAMB AND MUTTON

Lamb Stew

(LAMMFLEISCH RAGOUT)

Austria

2–3 *pounds stewing lamb*	2 *carrots*
Salt	2 *tablespoons butter*
8 *peppercorns*	2 *tablespoons flour*
2 *bay leaves*	Juice *of ½ lemon*
1 *medium onion*	

In a saucepan place the lamb cut up in small cubes. Barely
cover with cold water. Add salt, the peppercorns, bay leaves,
the whole onion, and the carrots, sliced lengthwise in half.
Bring to boil, cover with lid, and very slowly boil until meat is
tender. Strain but retain the cooking liquid.

In a separate saucepan heat the butter, lightly fry the flour
until golden, slowly add the cooking liquid of the stew. Stir
and let boil until it reaches the thickness of gravy. Put back
the meat, flavor with the lemon juice and serve, garnished with
mashed potatoes.
(Serves 6.)

Roast Leg of Lamb Esterházy Style

(BARANYCOMB ESTERHAZY MODRA)

Hungary

There is an anecdote according to which a nineteenth-century English duke would not believe that Hungarian lamb and mutton could compare to the English. Whereupon Prince Esterházy laid a bet with him that he had more shepherds than the duke had sheep. The prince won the bet, illustrating how plentiful and of what high quality this meat was, and is, in Hungary.

4 ounces larding bacon	4 tablespoons bacon fat
(or slices of bacon)	1 teaspoon Hungarian
1 leg of lamb	sweet red paprika
Salt	1 cup sour cream
Freshly ground black	
pepper	

Clean and lard the leg of lamb with the bacon. (If you have no larding needle, chop the bacon and scatter over the meat.) Add salt and pepper, set lamb in a roasting pan. Heat the 4 tablespoons of bacon fat until it boils and pour over the leg of lamb. Begin roasting in a 350° oven, basting it frequently. After half an hour, sprinkle top with red paprika and pour on the sour cream. Continue roasting slowly and basting the leg until meat is tender, about 1½ hours.
(Serves 6.)

Spring Lamb Cutlets

(MIEL)

Rumania

This excellent dish should be prepared only from the tenderest spring lamb chops. It is a Transylvanian specialty.

8 small spring lamb chops	Salt
1 cup milk	Freshly ground black
½ cup water	pepper
1 or 2 eggs	Lard or oil for deep-
Flour	frying
Finely sifted breadcrumbs	

Place the chops in a bowl and let soak for 2 hours in luke-warm milk diluted with water. Drain and dry well. Beat 1 or 2 eggs, depending on size of chops, as if for an omelet. Roll each chop in flour, dip into the beaten egg, and coat all over with the breadcrumbs. Add salt and pepper. Deep-fry until golden brown on both sides, drain and serve hot. The best garnish is VEGETABLE MARROW WITH DILL SAUCE. (Serves 4.)

Leg of Mutton Venison Style

(JAGNJETINA U LONCU)

Yugoslavia

1 leg of mutton	3 tomatoes, sliced
Salt	7 peppercorns
1 cup vinegar	Sprig of parsley
2 cups water	Thyme
3 bay leaves	1 tablespoon lard
2 medium onions, sliced	4 slices of bacon

Place the cleaned leg of mutton in an earthenware casserole. Rub with salt. Bring the vinegar and water to a boil and pour over the meat. Add bay leaves, onions, tomatoes, peppercorns, parsley, and thyme. Cover and keep in a cool place (but not in the refrigerator) for 24 hours.

Heat the lard in a large frying pan and quickly brown the leg of mutton on both sides. Take out the meat, cover it with the bacon, and put back in the casserole with the marinade. Cover with lid, place in a 350° oven, cook very slowly, reducing temperature to 250°, and then to 150°, for 1½ hours.

Strain the cooking liquid, slice the meat, and pour the sauce over it.

(Serves 6.)

Broad Beans with Lamb

(BORANIJA SA JAGNJETINOM)

Yugoslavia

1 *pound stewing lamb*	*Freshly ground black*
1 *pound fresh broad beans*	*pepper*
(or fresh Lima beans)	2 *tablespoons flour*
3 *tablespoons bacon fat*	1 *cup water*
2 *large onions, chopped*	2 *cloves garlic, crushed*
Salt	1 *cup yoghurt*

Cut the meat into cubes, leave the broad beans (or Lima beans) whole. In a saucepan heat the bacon fat, fry the chopped onion until golden. Add the cubed meat, fry on all sides till it changes color. Salt and pepper it, cover with lid, and begin stewing for 15 minutes. Now add the beans, a few spoonfuls of cold water, and continue stewing until meat is tender—about 1 hour.

Add the flour to the pan fat, stir, and fry for a few minutes. Dilute slowly with a cup of water. Add the crushed garlic, continue slowly boiling until gravy thickens. Lastly, just before serving, stir in the yoghurt. Heat but do not boil. (*Serves 6.*)

Mixed Skewered Meat

(RAZNJICI)

Yugoslavia

This is the Yugoslav version of the *kebab* or *shishkebab*. If served as a main course, allow 2 skewers per person. Always serve chopped raw onion on the side with this dish. The meat is best when it is charcoal-broiled or barbecued, but it can be made as well in the oven (not under an electric grill), where the skewers are put on a rack that is placed inside a roasting pan.

1 *pound beefsteak, cut in cubes*	Pepper
	5 *tablespoons bacon fat*
1 *pound stewing lamb, cut in cubes*	2 *tablespoons oil*
	Chopped onion
Salt	

Cut the two kinds of meat into inch-big cubes. Thread them, alternating beef and lamb, on small skewers. Salt and pepper them. Heat the bacon fat and the oil in a small saucepan. When warm, brush over the meat, and begin broiling slowly. Keep brushing them with the fat and turning skewers over so that the meat should cook evenly. Approximate cooking time is 20 minutes. Serve chopped onion separately on each plate.

(*Serves 8–10.*)

Mutton Goulash

(SZURETI GULYAS)

Hungary

Mutton goulash is a traditional dish prepared often in the open when the grape harvest is finished in the autumn. The new wine (*must* in Hungarian, *Heuriger* in Austria) is drunk with this pungent and tasty stew.

2 pounds stewing mutton	Salt
1 medium-sized onion	2 teaspoons caraway
4 tablespoons bacon fat	seeds (optional)
or lard	¾ pound potatoes
2 teaspoons Hungarian	4 cups water
sweet red paprika	

Cut meat into inch-large cubes. Finely chop the onion. In a stewing pan heat the fat or lard, fry the onion until golden, and sprinkle with the paprika. Put in the meat and fry over brisk heat until meat is browned on all sides. Add the salt, caraway seeds, a tablespoon of water, cover, and reduce heat to let meat stew very, very slowly. After 45 minutes, add the potatoes, peeled and cut lengthwise into quarters. Pour on the water, bring to boil, and cook until the potatoes and meat are both tender.
(*Serves 8.*)

Mutton Stew with Mushrooms

(ZADELAVANI JEHNECI)

Czechoslovakia

2 *pounds stewing mutton*	2 *tablespoons bacon fat*
Salt	*or butter*
5 *peppercorns*	1 *cup sliced fresh*
1 *onion*	*mushrooms*
2 *carrots*	2 *teaspoons chopped*
1 *stalk celery*	*parsley*
1 *bay leaf*	2 *tablespoons flour*

Cut mutton into small cubes. Place in a saucepan and cover with cold water. Add salt, peppercorns, and bring to boil. Reduce and let simmer very slowly for 20 minutes. Add the chopped onion, diced carrots, celery, and bay leaf. Continue gently boiling until meat is tender.

In a separate saucepan heat the fat or butter, add the sliced mushrooms and parsley. Cover and steam (without water) for 6 minutes. Take off lid, blend in the flour and slowly dilute with the cooking liquid of the mutton. Allow sauce to thicken, put back meat and the vegetables, and let cook, uncovered, for another 10 minutes.

Serve garnished with BREAD DUMPLINGS.

(*Serves 8.*)

Lamb Galantine

(DROP DE MIEL)

Rumania

This specialty is served at a formal Easter meal in Rumania. The dish is made from the stomach of a sheep, which is filled with the innards, sewn up to resemble a round ball, not unlike the *galantine* that the French make with chicken. It is preceded in Rumania by SHEEP'S-HEAD SOUP and is considered a great delicacy.

The lining of a sheep's stomach	2 teaspoons mixed thyme, basil (orégano)
The liver, kidneys, tongue of a sheep	1 or 2 egg yolks
Salt	2 tablespoons butter
Freshly ground black pepper	2 tablespoons cooking oil

Ask your specialty butcher to clean the sheep's stomach and prepare the lining for stuffing. Soak this in water for half an hour, then dry thoroughly.

Put the liver, kidneys, and tongue through the grinder. Season mixture with salt and pepper, add the herbs. Work into a smooth paste with the egg yolks. Spread over the stomach lining, shape like a ball, and sew up along the edges.

Well butter and oil a piece of greaseproof paper (or aluminum foil), wrap up the ball in it, taking care that no juice or fat should escape while baking it. Place inside a baking dish and bake in a 350° oven for 1½ hours.

Remove and discard the wrapping, serve sliced like a sausage. (*Serves 4–6.*)

Lamb with Spinach
(JACHNIA)
Bulgaria

1 *pound stewing lamb*	3 *tablespoons oil*
6 *spring onions*	*Salt*
2 *pounds fresh spinach*	*Freshly ground black*
(*or a 1-pound can of*	*pepper*
spinach)	1 *cup yoghurt*

Cut lamb into cubes and chop both white and green parts of the young spring onions. Clean spinach and wash in several waters. Drain and chop on a large chopping block.

In a deep saucepan heat the oil and fry the meat at brisk heat until lightly golden. Add the onions, salt and pepper, cover with lid, reduce heat, and let steam, very slowly, for 45 minutes. If necessary, add a spoonful of water at a time, when meat begins to stick to the pan.

Now add the spinach and cook together until meat is tender, about 15 more minutes. Lastly pour on the yoghurt, heat, but do not boil again.
(*Serves 6.*)

One-Course Meals, Garnishes, and Salads

A VILLAGE FAIR IN SLOVAKIA

Looking at the surface, that is, speaking geographically, there is nothing similar between the two countries. Slovakia—the southern part of Czechoslovakia, bordered by the Tatra Mountains in the north and by the Danube and Hungary in the south—is mountainous, thickly forested, and is six hundred miles from the nearest seaport. Whereas Ireland is just the opposite: flat, emerald green, and surrounded by the sea at the western extremities of Europe. And yet, to my imagination, at least, these two, Slovakia and Ireland, seem distant cousins. It has something to do with folklore, with mysticism and mysteries, with the way poteen can easily be mistaken, after the third or fourth glass, for *slivovic*, and a village church in Ireland for a village church in Slovakia.

You take the dirt road and follow the sound of bells: cowbells, sheep bells, or the bells ringing for the Angelus. At the road fork there is a cross wreathed with wilted wild flowers. In Slovakia it usually is the statue of a stone saint with a broken nose. Pure baroque. St. Nepomouk is his name, and he could have been Irish. Confessor to a queen, he chose martyrdom rather than divulge the secrets of his royal penitent. They flung him down from the bastions of the Hradcany, the royal palace in Prague. Today he is the patron saint of illiterate village folk and highly skilled diplomats as well. There is no logic to it: it is all a question of faith.

The people of Slovakia are humble and religious. The mountain woodcutter, the farmer who digs his steep potato fields that look like patchwork quilts as they slope down from the high forests above, the shepherd and the tinker, they all praise the Lord Jesus when meeting a stranger on the road. There are always processions; even if someone is dying the priest goes to his house in a procession followed by altar boys. There are Christmas processions with carol singers clad in shaggy sheepskin, and harvest processions when the fields are blessed and girls go in multicolored, many-layered skirts that swing to the rhythm of their steps. They wear ribbons in their hair that reach to their buttocks and sheafs of corn entwined with poppies to crown their heads. And almost every woman over forty is in black. Just like in Ireland, because in Slovakia mourning is also a perpetual state, disrupted only by death itself.

Down south and near the Hungarian border and the fertile plains, the village houses are whitewashed each spring. Roofs are made of thatch and geraniums bloom on the window sills.

Sunflowers keep up a struggling battle with the poplars, but no matter how high they grow, higher even than the wooden palings of the fence, they always lose and wilt their heads sadly at each sunset. Inside, the houses are mud-paved, and the place of honor in the "clean room," which gets used only on feast days or for funerals and weddings, perhaps, is for the faded photograph of a faraway son in Cincinnati or Philadelphia. Next to the Irish, the Slovaks are the world's greatest potato consumers. And also the most prolific immigrants.

The woodcutters seem to belong to a different race altogether. They live in the mountains all year round, coming in to the nearest village on holidays only. They are tall, silent men, standing around by themselves in the smoke-filled pubs, who fight only when they are provoked. They live in huts made of pinewood and twigs, and when they are not employed by a sawmill they burn wood for charcoal. As they move on, they abandon their huts, and you could follow their treks as you go hunting or roam the mountains of the Tatra. The woodcutters believe in fairies and the "little people" and out there, among the high peaks at night, cock a listening ear to the wailing sounds of ghosts. Their stories are never written down (illiteracy being a mark of distinction among them, handed down from generation to generation), just as the stories which go back to archaic times. Robbers and knights-errant, Turks and Tartars, and fair maidens strangled by the light of the first moon figure in their tales, where the past is intermingled with the present. They barter charcoal for sheep's cheese and bring down wood to the villages on rickety horse-drawn carts. The big logs are floated down the river in the form of rafts. Woodcutters who are engaged in this difficult transport, which requires great skill, are looked on as the aristocrats of the trade. They are like sailors as opposed to the infantry.

Once a month there is the big market and a fair, always on the main square of a different village. These draw large crowds from the mountains as well as from the whole district. Hawkers, horse and cattle dealers come from long distances, arriving usually during the night. First thing in the morning, before dawn breaks, the air is filled with the smell of burning charcoal and sizzling fat. Itinerant caterers who follow the markets set up their open-air kitchens within the precincts of the fairground. Flat potato cakes, crisp on the outside and soft inside, are the cheapest breakfast. Slightly more costly is the soup: goulash with plenty of potatoes, steaming hot, and ladled out to the accompaniment of voluminous sales talk by the cook, who seems to know each customer by name. There is competition as well as a secret fraternity among the market people. Father brings son while still young to learn the ropes, just the same as he had come with his father before. Children crowd around the open kitchens, buzzing like flies, flushed with the excitement of the coming day.

Near the horse dealers, a sharp and dandified group of men who wear cocky hats and long cavalry boots, hover the gypsy fortunetellers. They too follow the market, leaving their caravans, as ordered, strictly outside the boundaries of the village. The women still dress in long multilayered skirts, and flashy earrings dangle from their ears: they are almost invariably pregnant while another infant sucks at the breast. The horse dealers have the most money, and the gypsies know this, even if they cannot glimpse the wads of bank notes protruding from the pockets of their sheepskin jackets. The horse dealers do not go to the fair kitchens, but get served by errand boys who act as waiters for the stall keepers. They get plates and use their own knives, which they keep inside their boots. Whenever a successful deal is concluded, dealer and customer repair to the village pub together to celebrate. Here the gypsy musicians—a higher social group than the fortunetellers, since they have a fixed address and are no longer nomads—are playing already at ten in the morning. The spicy smell of sauerkraut and the mouth-watering odor of smoked and roast pork rise from the kitchen behind the restaurant. *Slivovic*, beer, white wine watered down with soda water are drunk in great quantities. The loyalty between Slovaks and Czechs is nowhere more apparent than over the zinc-lined counter at the bar where the Pilsener flows, blond and frothy like a spring river after the rains.

When the market is over, there still remains the fair with a merry-go-round, the shooting galleries, the candy-floss sellers and now and then the tattered and torn tent of a traveling circus which advertises its world-famous sword swallower from Malaya and monkeys to amuse the children. And late into the night the gypsies keep playing their old melodies, which know neither frontiers nor any distinction among race or creed and are timeless just like the Danube or the mountains.

ONE-COURSE MEALS

Mushroom Rice

(GOMBAS RIZS)

Hungary

This is my most successful garnish for a roast or breaded veal cutlets. When the rice is done this way, one can be completely sure that it will be fluffy.

2 cups long-grain rice
3 tablespoons butter
½ pound fresh or
    cultivated mushrooms,
    chopped
Salt

Freshly ground black
    pepper
3 cups cold canned
    bouillon or stock
2 tablespoons chopped
    parsley

Do not wash rice. In a saucepan heat the butter and fry the rice for a few minutes. Do not brown. Finely chop the mushrooms and add to the rice. Salt and pepper to taste. Pour over it the cold bouillon or stock (if neither is available, use cold water and add a bouillon cube—very satisfactory!). Cover with lid, bring to boil, and immediately reduce heat. Let rice simmer for 10 to 12 minutes. Add the chopped parsley, and cook one more minute.
(*Serves 6.*)

Meat Pie

(BUREK)

Yugoslavia

Meat pies in Yugoslavia (and indeed in all Balkan countries) differ from our pies in that they are made with alternate layers of filling and pastry. It is important to remember, therefore, to cook these pies slowly, since nothing is worse than to bite into uncooked pastry in the middle of a pie.

Oil	*¾ pound stewing beef,*
1 *pound* BASIC	*ground*
UNSWEETENED PUFF	*Salt*
PASTE	*Freshly ground black*
1 *medium red onion,*	*pepper*
finely chopped	*1 egg*
¾ pound stewing pork,	*Egg yolk to brush top*
ground	*with*

Grease a deep pie dish or cake tin with oil. Divide pastry into 4 parts and roll out each to the thickness of a piecrust.

Fry the minced onion in a little oil, and after a few minutes add the ground pork and beef. Fry, stirring and mixing very well, for 5 minutes. Add salt and plenty of black pepper. Transfer to a mixing bowl and mix in the egg so that mixture becomes a smooth paste.

Line bottom of pie dish with the pastry. Spread some of the meat mixture on top, then cover with the second layer of pastry. Continue alternating filling and pastry till all ingredients

are used up. Top layer is pastry, of course. Brush with a little
beaten egg yolk.

Start in a 400° oven, then after a few minutes reduce heat
to 300°. Bake pie for 45 minutes.
(*Serves 6.*)

Cheese Pie

(GIBANICA)

Yugoslavia

For this pie, which is an excellent supper dish or can serve
as a first course, the Greek *feta* cheese is used. It is made of
sheep's milk and has a firm, smooth texture. *Feta* cheese is
now available at specialty food shops.

Olive oil	*Salt*
Double recipe of BASIC	*Ground pepper*
SHORT PASTRY	*Beaten egg yolk*
1 *pound* feta *cheese*	
(*or fresh* mozzarella	
cheese)	

Take a round cake tin, at least 4 inches deep, and oil the inside well. Divide the pastry into 3 parts, roll each out thinly.
Slice *feta* or *mozzarella* cheese very thin.

Line the tin with pastry, cover with sliced cheese. Salt and
pepper it. Now cover with the second layer of pastry, then
again cheese, salt and pepper. The top layer should be pastry,
which is brushed with a little beaten egg yolk. Preheat oven

to 450° and put in the pie. After 10 minutes reduce temperature to 300° and bake for 30 minutes more. Should the top get too well done, it is advisable to cover with some greaseproof paper or aluminum foil.

The important thing is to start this pie in a hot oven but then cook it slowly in order to get the pastry well done. (*Serves 4.*)

Eggplant Casserole

(IMAM BAJALDO)

Bulgaria

5 large eggplants	Salt
Flour	Pepper
Oil for deep-frying	1 cup hot water
3 red onions	
5 tablespoons chopped parsley	

Wash but do not peel the eggplants and slice them in rounds the thickness of a finger. Roll them in flour, and deep-fry in hot oil till crisp and golden.

Grease an ovenproof casserole and line with eggplant slices. Sprinkle with finely chopped onion and parsley. Season with salt and pepper. Cover with another layer of fried eggplant, similarly sprinkle with onion and parsley, and season. Continue till all ingredients are used up.

Pour a cup of hot water over the mixture and put in a 350° oven. Bake until all liquid is absorbed and serve either hot or cold. (*Serves 6.*)

Egg and Cottage Cheese Omelet

(KAJMAK SA JAJAIMA-MOCA)

Yugoslavia

In Yugoslavia they make a cottage cheese that is preserved in a wooden container and is called *kajmak*. Traveling in the country, one can always count on finding the *kajmak* and fresh homemade bread at a farmhouse. This bread with a thick slice of cottage cheese is one of the great simple joys in life. The egg and cottage cheese omelet given here is the Yugoslav version of the Swiss fondue. It is eaten from a common frying pan that is placed in the middle of the table, and everybody tucks in and helps himself.

To Make Cottage Cheese (the Kajmak):

It is important that fresh, unpasteurized cow's milk should be used. Take a pint of milk and pour it into a deep saucepan. Cook at the lowest possible temperature on top of the stove for 1 hour. The cream that has formed on top is now taken off carefully and conserved in a wooden container in the refrigerator or a very cool place. Each day a fresh layer is added, with only a little salt between each layer to flavor the cheese. This is the cottage cheese or *kajmak*.

Egg and Cheese Omelet:

2 eggs per person	Cottage cheese to cover
Salt	surface of frying pan
Cooking fat	1 onion (optional)

Beat eggs with half a teaspoon of lukewarm water to each egg. Lightly salt. Grease a large frying pan and when hot pour in the egg mixture. Immediately cover with quarter-inch-thick layer of cottage cheese. Reduce heat and let the eggs set. Serve directly from the pan.

Sometimes a fried onion is mixed in with the eggs.

Pancakes for Basic Use

2 cups flour	1⅔ cups milk
2 eggs	Butter or bacon fat for
¼ teaspoon salt	frying

Put the flour in a mixing bowl. Make a hole in the middle and put in the eggs and salt. With a wooden spoon, blend flour with eggs. Now slowly, while steadily beating, add the milk. The mixture should have the thickness of cream.

In a heavy iron frying pan, which you grease with a little bacon fat or butter before making each pancake, pour in about 3 tablespoonfuls of the mixture. Fry at strong heat first on one side, then on the other.

Fill, according to recipes given.

(*This mixture yields about 8–10 pancakes.*)

Paprika Pancakes

(PAPRIKAS PALACSINTA)

Hungary

These pancakes were the specialty of a very romantic little restaurant in the old part of Buda, called The Marble Bride. There, in summertime, one ate in the courtyard under cen-

turies-old trees, and strolling gypsies played melancholy tunes
to go with the exquisite food.

8 PANCAKES FOR BASIC USE	1 *pound stewing veal*
½ *small red onion, finely chopped*	*Salt*
	1 *tablespoon flour*
	½ *cup sour cream*
2 *tablespoons bacon fat, lard or butter*	*Butter*
1 *teaspoon Hungarian sweet red paprika*	

First prepare your pancakes, which you may do even the day
before and keep, wrapped in aluminum foil, in the refrigerator.

Very finely chop the onion and fry in the fat till golden.
Sprinkle with red paprika, put in the meat, which should be
cut into cubes first and then chopped into very small pieces
(not minced, however, just chopped). Fry the meat in the
onion fat at brisk heat, stirring all the time. Now salt, and
then cover with a lid, reducing heat to a bare simmer. Do not
add water, but let it cook very gently for half an hour. Dust
with the flour, stir and fry a few minutes, then lastly, off the
fire, blend in the sour cream.

Fill each pancake with this veal paprika, roll up and place
on a well-greased ovenproof dish. Dot top with butter pieces,
moisten with sour cream, and bake for 15 minutes in a 400°
oven.

If pancakes and fillings are made the same day and are still
warm, it is enough to put the filled pancakes under the broiler
for a few minutes before serving.
(*Serves 4.*)

Savory Layer Pancakes

(RAKOTT PALACSINTA)

Hungary

This is my favorite first course, which earns praise even at formal dinner parties. Why I like it especially is that one can make it the day before, even though the base is pancakes, and needs only to be reheated in the oven before serving.

12 PANCAKES FOR BASIC	Salt
USE	Freshly ground black
4 tablespoons butter	pepper
2 tablespoons flour	8 ounces cooked ham,
1 cup milk	finely chopped
2 ounces grated Parmesan	8 ounces mushrooms,
cheese	chopped and cooked
2 egg yolks	

Prepare pancakes. Take a round, deep ovenproof dish that can also go to the table. Grease it well.

Prepare a thick white sauce from 2 tablespoons butter, the flour, and the cup of milk. Remove from flame, add the grated Parmesan cheese, and one by one blend in the egg yolks. Add salt and pepper. Add ham to the cheese sauce. Do not cook any more. Toss the finely chopped mushrooms in a little butter for a few minutes.

Line the bottom of the dish with a pancake. Spread with ham and cheese sauce. Cover with a pancake. Sprinkle with the mushrooms. Continue with alternate fillings till all the ingredients are used up. Top layer should be pancake.

Dot the top liberally with pieces of the remaining butter

(you may also spread with thick sour cream). Put in a 350°
oven (covered with a piece of aluminum foil) and bake for
25 minutes.

Serve directly from dish and cut in cake wedges.
(*Serves 6–8.*)

Brain Croquettes

(HIRNPALATSCHINKEN)
Austria

This dish is an exquisite first course and is served with TARTARE
SAUCE. In general, 2 croquettes are served per person. The
base is pancakes, prepared without sugar.

8–10 PANCAKES FOR BASIC USE

The Filling:

2 *cups brains* (*calf,*	2 *teaspoons parsley*
sheep, beef)	1 *tablespoon flour*
2 *tablespoons butter*	½ *cup canned bouillon*
Salt	*or water*
Freshly ground black	2 *eggs, beaten*
pepper	*Breadcrumbs*

Clean the brains thoroughly and chop them finely. Heat butter in a saucepan, put in brains, salt, pepper, parsley, cover,
and steam for 6 minutes. Blend in the flour, fry for a few
minutes, dilute with bouillon or water, and let cook, uncovered
for 4 more minutes. Spread cooked and creamed brains on each
pancake. Roll up, tuck in edges, dip in beaten egg, then
breadcrumbs, and fry in butter or fat till golden brown. Serve
with TARTARE SAUCE.
(*Serves 4–6.*)

Bread-Roll Dumplings

(SEMMELKNODERLN)

Austria

3 bread rolls	Pinch of nutmeg
1½ tablespoons melted	2 eggs
bacon fat or lard	1 cup lukewarm water
3 cups flour	3 tablespoons sour cream
Salt	

Use a few-days-old bread rolls (the Austrian *Semmel*). Cut into slices, then cut slices into very small squares. Heat bacon fat or lard in a frying pan and fry bread squares until crisp and golden. Remove and drain fat from them.

Put the flour in a mixing bowl. Add salt, nutmeg, and the fried bread squares. Beat the eggs and slowly, stirring with a wooden spoon, add to the mixture. Now pour in, little by little, the lukewarm water, beating hard to achieve a smooth, soft dough.

Lightly dust your hands with flour and shape round dumplings, about 2 inches in diameter, from the mixture. (Always make the dumplings small, as they grow in size during cooking.) Heat plenty of salted water, and when it boils, drop in the dumplings one by one. Do not cover, but keep water gently boiling. Cook for 10 to 15 minutes. Drain and run some cold water over them.

Add the sour cream to the fat in the frying pan, heat, and put in the dumplings. Roll them in this fat with a spoon for a few minutes and serve.

(*Serves* 6.)

Egg Dumplings

(NOKI OR NOKKERLI)

Hungary

These very small dumplings serve as the classical garnish for chicken or veal paprika or the *pörkölts*, which are the Hungarian stews with a paprika gravy. The smaller the dumplings, the greater the praise for the cook's skill.

2½ cups flour	⅓–½ cup lukewarm water
1 egg	Bacon fat, lard, or butter
Salt	to toss them in

Put the flour in a mixing bowl. Break in egg, add salt. With the help of a wooden spatula, beat till egg is well blended with the flour.

Now, slowly, and beating steadily, pour in the lukewarm

water. The mixture should have the thickness of a soft scone dough. Rinse a large wooden slab with cold water. Have plenty of salted water ready and boiling.

Take a teaspoon, dip it into the boiling water. Put half of the dough mixture on the slab and with the edge of the spoon cut small dumplings directly in the boiling water. When dumplings have risen to the surface, they are done.

Strain and rinse under cold water. Meanwhile in a saucepan heat a little bacon fat or butter, toss in the dumplings, stir, and heat for a few minutes. Serve at once.
(*Serves 6.*)

Potato Dumplings

(BRAMBOROVE KNEDLIKY)

Czechoslovakia

Potato dumplings the size of a tennis ball are another well-known garnish with stews and meats. It should be noted here that in order to achieve the correct result you must use potatoes that were boiled the day before. Also, do not allow the dough to rest, but cook it immediately, since standing will make the dumplings soft.

1½ *pounds potatoes*	*Salt*
3 *cups flour*	2 *eggs*

Boil potatoes in their skin 24 hours in advance. Peel and let cool. When ready to prepare dumplings, pass potatoes through a sieve. Add flour, salt, and the eggs one by one. Knead by hand until the mixture is smooth. Shape into balls and drop into boiling salted water. Cook for 15 minutes, drain, and serve at once. (*Serves 6.*)

Bread Dumplings

(HUSKOVE KNEDLIKY)

Czechoslovakia

One of the greatest contributions of Czech cooking is its dumplings. A large variety is known in Czechoslovakia, but the most popular are the bread dumplings, which are served as a garnish to roast pork, to stews with a rich gravy, to game. These dumplings have the shape of a thick sausage about three inches in diameter and are cut, when cooked, with a thread into one-inch-thick slices.

4 cups unsifted flour	¾ cup water
Salt	2 egg yolks
1 cup milk	5 slices stale white bread

In a large mixing bowl put in the flour and salt. Take a wooden spatula and little by little beat in the milk mixed with the water. Separately beat the egg yolks and beat in those too. (An electric mixer can be used.) Keep beating until the dough is well mixed and separated from the edge of the bowl.

It is very important to use bread a few days old. Cut into very small squares, and when the dough is right, fold them in gently. Divide mixture into 3 parts. Shape each part like an oblong sausage.

Heat plenty of salted water in a large, deep saucepan. When the water boils, put in the dumplings. Do not cover, but let water simmer very gently. Cook for half an hour. Drain.

Cut into slices with strong thread. Serve warm.

(Serves 6.)

Creamed Spinach

(SPINATPURE)

Austria

2 pounds fresh spinach	1 tablespoon flour
(or one large can)	Salt
1 cup milk	Freshly ground black
2 thin slices white bread	pepper
2 tablespoons butter	Pinch of nutmeg
1 or 2 cloves garlic,	(optional)
crushed	

Remove stems from the spinach, wash in several waters. Let spinach boil in salted water for no more than 5 minutes. Drain but retain some of the cooking liquid.

Soak the bread roll or bread in a little milk, then squeeze out. Add to spinach and put both through a grinder (or cream in an electric blender).

In a saucepan heat the butter, add the garlic, fry for only a minute. Blend in the flour, stir and fry for a few minutes. Dilute with the milk to the thickness of a very thick white sauce. Now add the creamed spinach, season with salt and black pepper, stir and mix thoroughly and let it boil, uncovered, for 5 to 10 more minutes. If purée is too thick, moisten with a little of the spinach water.

If you prefer more garlic, you may add it to taste. In Austria, they flavor the spinach with a little nutmeg.

(*Serves 6–8 as a garnish.*)

Vegetable Marrow with Dill Sauce

(TOKFOZELEK)

Hungary

This is perhaps one of the most typical of the spring-summer vegetable garnishes in Hungary. It accompanies roasts, hamburgers, breaded lamb chops, or is just enjoyed on its own on account of its fragrant flavor. At Hungarian markets the already shredded vegetable marrow is sold by the pound, the same as sauerkraut that one buys directly from the barrel.

The vegetable marrow (or squash) used in Hungary is large (it can be very large, weighing several pounds), is gourd-shaped, and has a white skin and flesh. To preserve it for winter, good housewives bottle it, already shredded, between layers of coarse salt.

1–2 *pounds vegetable*	1 *cup sour cream*
marrow (large zucchini	2 *tablespoons flour*
or summer squash)	¼ *cup canned bouillon*
2 *tablespoons butter*	1 *teaspoon sugar*
Fresh or powdered dill	2 *teaspoons vinegar*
Salt	

Peel the marrow, cut lengthwise into halves, and scoop out all seeds, very finely shred in long, spaghetti-like shapes. Put in a large dish and liberally sprinkle all over with salt. Let stand, covered, for half an hour, then squeeze between your hands, to get rid of all liquid.

In a saucepan heat the butter, add the dill, salt (but carefully), cover, and steam the shredded marrow. Do not add any water. Meanwhile in a mixing bowl blend the sour cream with the flour and bouillon. When marrow is cooked (about 10 minutes), pour the cream mixture over it, let it come to a boil, uncovered. Let simmer, very gently for a few minutes, then add sugar, vinegar and serve warm.

In summer, chilled, this dish is very refreshing. (*Serves 6.*)

String Beans Au Gratin

(ZOLDBAB FOZELEK)

Hungary

1 *pound string beans*	4 *tablespoons butter*
1 *teaspoon sugar*	½ *cup fresh white*
1 *teaspoon wine vinegar*	*breadcrumbs*
Salt	½ *cup sour cream*
Freshly ground black	
pepper	

Boil string beans in salted water to which you add a spoonful of sugar and 1 of vinegar. Cook for 15 minutes, no more. Drain.

Butter a deep, round casserole and put in beans. Season with salt and pepper.

In a frying pan heat the butter, pour this over the beans. Sprinkle top with ⅓ of the breadcrumbs generously, and spread the sour cream over them. Sprinkle remaining breadcrumbs on top.

Put casserole into a 350° oven and bake for 10 minutes or until breadcrumbs on top are golden. (*Serves 4–6.*)

Stewed Peppers

(LECSO)

Hungary

2 *medium-sized onions*	*Salt*
4 *or 5 green peppers*	*Freshly ground black*
1 *pound fresh tomatoes*	*pepper*
(or canned whole	2 *eggs (use frankfurters*
tomatoes)	*or dry Hungarian*
2 *or 3 tablespoons bacon*	*paprika sausages as an*
fat or lard	*alternative to eggs)*

Finely chop or slice the onions. Seed and dice the green peppers. Peel and quarter tomatoes.

In a heavy frying pan heat the bacon fat or lard and fry the onions until light gold. Add the diced peppers, salt, and cover with lid. Reduce heat and let stew for 10 minutes. Add the tomatoes now, some freshly ground black pepper, and let the mixture slowly stew, covered, for half an hour or more.

The vegetables should resemble a thick purée. If you find that too much liquid is left after stewing tomatoes, take off the lid, increase heat, and boil off the surplus.

Beat eggs with a fork, pour over the stew, stir with a fork just as you do when scrambling eggs. After 3 minutes serve at once.

Should you prefer it, leave out the eggs, and add frankfurters or dry Hungarian paprika sausages to the stew when adding tomatoes. They should be added when the stew is almost done, since they require very little cooking.

(*Serves 4–6.*)

Cucumbers in Casserole

(MUSSAKA)

Bulgaria

Mussaka is a vegetable-and-meat casserole known all through the Balkans. It is a one-course meal, and in Bulgaria either cucumbers or eggplants are used.

1 *onion*	*Flour*
4 *tablespoons oil*	*Salt*
¾ *pound ground beef*	*Freshly ground black*
2 *or 3 fresh tomatoes*	*pepper*
(or canned, peeled	½ *teaspoon Hungarian*
whole tomatoes)	*sweet red paprika*
4 *or 5 medium-sized green*	3 *eggs*
cucumbers	

Finely chop onion and fry in a little oil together with the ground meat. Peel and quarter tomatoes and add to the pan, letting them fry together with meat and onions for 10 minutes.

Meanwhile peel cucumbers and slice. Dip them in flour, heat some more oil in a separate pan, and quickly fry cucumbers on both sides until golden and crisp. Prepare a well-oiled, deep casserole, make layers alternating the fried cucumbers with the meat and tomato mixture. Season with salt, pepper, and red paprika. The top layer should be cucumbers. Bake in a 375° oven for 20 minutes.

Beat the eggs with a fork as if for an omelet, pour over the cucumber casserole, and return to oven for 5 minutes to allow eggs to set like a custard. Serve hot or cold. (*Serves 4–6.*)

Baked Potato Casserole

(RAKOTT BURGONYA)
Hungary

This very popular dish is much more than a simple garnish: it could serve as a one-course meal or as a supper dish, accompanied with tossed green salad.

6 large boiled potatoes	Pepper
3 or 4 hard-cooked eggs	4 tablespoons butter
2–4 pairs of frankfurters	1 cup sour cream
or Polish dry sausage	Breadcrumbs
Salt	

Boil potatoes in their skins, then peel and slice in thin, round discs. (Take care to keep the potatoes a little undercooked, otherwise they break easily.) Slice eggs similarly and cut up frankfurters or sausage.

Take a deep casserole and butter it well. Start with making a layer of potatoes. Salt and pepper it and stud with little pieces of butter. Scatter with a few sausages and pieces of egg, then cover with a layer of potatoes. This time, after seasoning it, spread potatoes with sour cream. Follow with eggs, sausage again, and moisten generously with either butter or sour cream. The last layer is always potatoes, which are then sprinkled with breadcrumbs, dotted with pieces of butter, and finished off with cream.

Bake in a 350° oven for 20 to 30 minutes and serve directly from casserole.
(*Serves 6.*)

Baked Maize

(MAMALIGA LA CUPTOR)

Rumania

Maize cooked in the same way as our porridge is a much-loved and famous dish in Rumania. The *mamaliga* is offered either on its own (from the oven—*la cuptor*) or as a garnish with stews.

3 *cups water*	½ *cup of sour cream*
Salt	4 *slices of feta* (*Greek*)
1 *cup corn meal*	*cheese*
2 *tablespoons butter*	4 *eggs*

Bring salted water to boil and add the corn meal. Cook like a porridge, by stirring very frequently with a wooden spoon, for 25 minutes.

Well butter a deep ovenproof casserole that can go directly
to the table. Pour in the thick porridge. Cover with the sour
cream and arrange the thin slices of *feta* cheese on top. Put
in 400° oven or under the broiler for 10 minutes.

Separately poach the eggs, and when the *mamaliga* is golden
on top, garnish with 1 poached egg per person.
(*Serves 4.*)

Egg and Yoghurt Pie

Bulgaria

This pie, made without a pastry crust, is a Bulgarian specialty
that can be eaten hot or cold, cut in cake wedges. For the
cheese I use a strong, dry Gruyère.

½ cup oil	2 teaspoons chopped
5 cups yoghurt	parsley
6 eggs	4 level tablespoons finely
Salt	sifted breadcrumbs
Freshly ground black	½ pound Gruyère cheese
pepper	2 cups milk

Oil a deep round pie pan. In a mixing bowl put in the yoghurt.
Beat in the eggs one by one. Add salt and pepper and the
chopped parsley. Mix in the breadcrumbs and the cheese,
which should be coarsely grated. Pour this mixture into the
baking pan, cover with milk, and bake in a 350° oven for
25 minutes.
(*Serves 6.*)

Scrambled Eggs Hungarian Style

(SZALONNAS RANTOTTA)

Hungary

6 eggs	1 medium-sized red onion,
6 teaspoons lukewarm	finely chopped
water	1 teaspoon Hungarian
Salt	sweet red paprika
4 ounces larding bacon	
or Hungarian szalonna	

In a bowl beat eggs with the lukewarm water and season with salt. Cut the larding bacon (or Hungarian *szalonna*, available in Hungarian food shops) into very small cubes.

In a heavy iron frying pan put in the bacon, at low heat fry till all the fat is let out. Remove the pieces of crisp bacon and keep warm.

In the same frying pan fry the onion till golden. Immediately pour the eggs over them and scramble until set. Mix in the fried bacon pieces or scatter them on top.

Dust top before serving with paprika.
(*Serves 4.*)

Mushroom Paprika

(PAPRIKAS GOMBA)

Hungary

1½ pounds fresh
  mushrooms
½ small red onion
1½ tablespoons bacon fat
1 teaspoon Hungarian
  sweet red paprika
Salt

Freshly ground black
  pepper
2 tablespoons flour
¾ cup canned bouillon
  or water
4 or 5 tablespoons sour
  cream

Wash and slice the mushrooms, finely chop the onion. In a saucepan heat the fat and fry the onions until golden. Blend in paprika and put in the sliced mushrooms immediately. Cover with lid, reduce heat, and let mushrooms stew in their own juice for 10 minutes. Add salt and pepper, blend in the flour with the gravy, stir and fry for a few minutes. Dilute with bouillon or cold water and let boil, uncovered for 6 more minutes. Lastly, off the fire, add the sour cream to the paprika sauce.

(Serves 4.)

GARNISHES

Risotto

Though a typically Italian dish, the *risotto* is adopted in the Austro-Hungarian kitchen and used mainly as a side dish. In Italy, *risotto* is served as a first course, starting off a meal like a dish of spaghetti or a minestrone.

Two ingredients are essential for a *risotto:* the bouillon in which the rice is cooked and the saffron which colors it yellow. Dry, uncooked rice is started off in a generous amount of butter where it gets fried first. Then the bouillon is added, always in small quantities, while the cook must stir the mixture with a wooden spoon, never covering the saucepan with a lid. The saffron is added 5 minutes before the rice is cooked, which never takes more or less than 20 minutes.

2 *cups of dry, uncooked rice*	*Pinch of salt*
	4 *cups canned bouillon*
3 *tablespoons butter*	¼ *teaspoon saffron*

In a saucepan heat the butter and dry-fry rice for 5 minutes, stirring all the time. Moisten with a cup of bouillon (add salt, if canned bouillon is unsalted only!), reduce heat to a low simmer, stir, and cook until moisture is absorbed. Then pour on more bouillon and continue cooking as above. With the last cup of bouillon add the saffron. Cooking time is 20 minutes.
(This quantity should serve as a garnish with meat for 6 people.)

SALADS

Fresh Cucumber Salad

(UBORKASALATA)

Hungary

In Hungary this is one of the favorite salads, used as a garnish with chicken fried in breadcrumbs, with *Wiener schnitzel*, and with roast goose. Since cucumbers are rather difficult to digest, it is important to prepare them always a day in advance, by letting them stand in salt and then squeezing out all the juice.

3 *firm green cucumbers*	½ *teaspoon sugar*
Salt	1 *teaspoon Hungarian*
2 *tablespoons white wine*	*sweet red paprika*
vinegar	

Peel cucumbers and slice very thin. Put in a china or glass bowl and liberally sprinkle with salt. Cover and let stand overnight.

Now take the cucumbers and squeeze them hard by hand, getting rid of all surplus liquid that formed overnight. Transfer to a salad bowl, dress with the white wine vinegar to which a little sugar is added, and sprinkle top with paprika. Serve chilled.

(*Serves 4.*)

Eggplant Salad or Mock Caviar

(KOPELO)

Bulgaria

You will encounter this dish all over the Near and Middle East. It is a salad made with eggplants, but it resembles caviar, which is why in Rumania they call it mock caviar.

3 or 4 firm, medium-sized eggplants	Salt
4–6 tablespoons salad or olive oil	Freshly ground black pepper
2 tablespoons white wine vinegar	3 cloves garlic, crushed (or 1 onion, minced)

Roast eggplants in a hot oven over a rack. When outer-skin begins to flake and is black all over, take out and peel. Place eggplants in a large mixing bowl. With a wooden spoon crush the eggplant by beating, and when it becomes a pulp, slowly, while still beating, pour in the oil and the vinegar. Now add the salt and pepper, mix in the crushed garlic or, if preferred, the finely minced onion. Let chill thoroughly in the refrigerator before serving. (Serves 6–8.)

Hot Chilli Preserve

(AJVAR)

Yugoslavia

This is the Yugoslav version of a chutney (or even stronger in resemblance to the Indonesian *sambal*), only it is made with hot chillies, tomatoes, eggplant, and plenty of garlic. It can be preserved in jars, and is used invariably with those delightful YUGOSLAV BROILED BEEF SAUSAGES, *cevapcici*.

2 medium-sized eggplants	Freshly ground black
4 green peppers	pepper
1 pound fresh, ripe	4 or 5 sharp, fresh hot
tomatoes	chillies
4 cloves garlic	½ cup olive oil
2 onions	3 tablespoons vinegar
Salt	

Put peppers and eggplants on a rack and roast them in a hot oven. When the skin is black, carefully peel off the outer layer. If you do not want this condiment to be very hot, you may also discard the seeds of the peppers.

Peel tomatoes and crush the garlic. Put the onions, peppers, eggplant and tomatoes through a grinder (or in a blender). You should obtain a smooth, pulpy mixture. Add salt, plenty of black pepper, and the chillies, mix together with the oil and vinegar.

Ajvar is eaten fresh, but it can also be bottled and steamed to preserve for the winter.

Green Pepper Mayonnaise

(PAPRIKASALATA)

Hungary

This exquisite salad was given to me by a friend who calls it "Vilma salad," after his mother. I serve it always with great success at cold buffets.

4 or 5 fresh green peppers	Salt
1 cup water	Freshly ground black
2 teaspoons sugar	pepper
3 tablespoons white wine	1 cup mayonnaise
vinegar	

Put peppers on a rack and roast in hot oven until the outer skin begins to blister and turn black. Remove and peel off the black skin.

Discard the seeds and cut peppers into thin, long strips. Put in a china bowl and pour over them 1 cup of water to which you added 2 teaspoons of sugar and the white wine vinegar. Salt and pepper and cover and let stand overnight in this liquid. Drain thoroughly and mix with mayonnaise. Let chill in refrigerator before serving.

(Serves 4–6.)

Cold Brain Salad

(SALATA DE CREER)

Rumania

In Rumania they serve this dish very cold and call it salad, since its consistency is not unlike a Russian mayonnaise salad. It can be used as a party dish for buffet suppers with great effect.

6 sheep's brains (or 4
  calf's brains)
1 cup water
Salt
Sprig of parsley
2 medium red onions,
  minced

Ground white pepper
2–3 tablespoons salad
  or olive oil
Juice of 1 lemon

Clean brains under running cold water. Place in a saucepan with a cup of water, salt, a sprig of parsley. Boil gently for 15 minutes.

Drain and clean off any remaining dark blood vessels. Brains must be very thoroughly cleaned and white.

Put brains in a wooden salad bowl, add the onion, a little more salt, and white pepper. With a wooden spoon, while adding slowly the oil and lemon juice, work the brains into a smooth, creamy paste. Place in refrigerator and let paste chill thoroughly.

(Serves 6–8.)

Cakes and Desserts

THE HOUSE WITH THE FOUR LARDERS

Back in Hungary, where I lived as a child, we had a house with four larders. Each larder was locked like the treasure chambers in Grimm's fairy tales, and my grandmother kept their keys in her wicker basket, where she also kept her spectacles and knitting. She was not, however, a saucer-eyed monster out of Grimm, but a sweet, fragile old lady dressed in ankle-length black mourning. From morning to night she was busy running a small household of three with the aid of seven servants.

In Larder Number One, our daily provisions were kept, from which Grandmother gave out each morning the cook's daily needs. There was also an enormous ice chest in this room, resembling a Roman sarcophagus and large enough to hold the body of a giant. Water was dripping from it steadily into an enamel basin and enormous blocks of ice were delivered daily to our door by a husky gypsy, the iceman.

In the second room, for which there was a separate key and where the cook was forbidden to enter after her, Grandmother kept the bulk provisions. The room was fitted out with shelves and deep drawers, just like a provincial grocery store. On the red-tiled floor rested bags full of flour, rice, haricot beans, split peas, walnuts, and sugar. In the drawers were pounds and pounds of sultana raisins, poppy seeds, while dark blocks of confectioner's chocolate were kept in readiness to be used for the cakes and sweets that were baked each day.

Not that we lived in the country, where in the winter one may expect to be snowed in and unable to go out to the nearest store. We lived right in the center of a busy town and the grocery boy called each morning for cook's urgent needs, which in spite of the four full larders were always quite considerable.

Tea was ordered directly from a firm in London, from where it arrived in beautiful ten-pound boxes decorated with Chinese orange blossom and pictures of robed ladies with parasols strolling among pagodas. Coffee from Brazil came from a Viennese importer, cocoa directly from Holland, and spaghetti from Italy. There were household accounts to be paid in four languages.

I loved the spicy smell of the second larder, but what I loved even more was to follow Grandmother to the next sanctuary—the smoking room, she called it, not because it was there that Grandfather could smoke his pipe or cigars, but because of the smoked small goods stored in there. In this room one entered as in a cathedral with eyes lifted toward the ceiling: hung from wires strung across the room were whole hams, sausages, sides of bacon, and other mouth-watering delicacies. On the brick floor rested huge earthenware jars containing the lard used for our cooking. No self-respecting housewife would ever buy the lard from the butcher: it had to be melted out at home and preferably made of home-cured bacon.

In this third room on the window sill, on a blue and white onion-patterned Meissen plate, nestled the inevitable goose liver, which I liked best for breakfast, with its golden fat spread on a bread roll and nice chunks of crisply fried liver put on top. Goose liver was such a commonplace in Hungary that even during the war we seldom went without it, and as for *pâtés*, one had at least two kinds of them handy at home— goose liver *pâté* and game pie, and often a little chicken gelatine as well for variation.

The fourth and last of the larders resembled a pharmacy, with rows and rows of shelves reaching to the ceiling, each with carefully labeled bottles containing the preserves. Beginning with the first cherries in early summer and ending with the tomatoes in August, everything that could be picked and was edible was also bottled at home. Strawberries for jam, whole strawberries in brandy, apricots, peaches, plums, and pears, candied melon rind and transparent orange marmalade in jars, small or large, tall or narrow, screw-topped or tight up with transparent cellophane paper and each labeled in Grandmother's script with the date underneath. The reason why at my age I still have occasional trouble with a complicated can opener is because way back in those prewar years in Hungary the only can I saw in our house was of sardines . . . the finest French sardines, of course, imported from Paris.

As a rule, one or two uniced cakes and dozens and dozens of cookies and biscuits were also kept in the fourth larder on large wire racks. We had sweets with every meal, always homemade and seldom the same one the next day and extra cakes were always ready in case unexpected visitors arrived and pressed to stay for lunch or dinner, huge meals, after which closer friends were given the beds or couches in our guest rooms to lie down for a siesta.

And yet the curious thing that remains in my memory was not this abundance of food, which people in Hungary took for granted. It was to do with vanilla crescents and *Ischler* cakes. Those Grandmother never kept in the larder. No sooner were they made than she took a long, rectangular silver tray, placed a hand-crocheted doily for protection over the surface, and arranged the cookies with great symmetry on top. With this tray she then walked into her bedroom, where two immense walnut wardrobes stood facing the beds. One wardrobe for the dresses, the other for the linen. In the second one every single item was placed between pink tissue paper sheets and tied up with a blue satin ribbon with her initials embroidered on each.

She put the tray with the vanilla crescents and *Ischlers* on the third shelf, on top of a neat pile of damask table napkins. Each afternoon when she would wake from her nap, Grandmother would call me in her room and, unlocking the linen closet, would offer me a cookie. She called it "something to bite between your teeth." It has become such a habit that today I cannot wake from my sleep without looking toward the closet in my room in the hope of finding there "something to bite."

CAKES

Vanilla-Flavored Powdered Sugar

On the Continent, when vanilla is called for as flavoring, vanilla bean is meant and not the bottled essence. Vanilla bean is available at specialty shops, and for baking one uses a small piece (about an inch long). The bean is split open lengthwise and the fine vanilla powder scraped out. It is customary to leave also the shell in the mixture, but it should be removed always, before serving.

To Preserve the Vanilla Bean:

One should keep it in a tightly closed jar, embedded in sugar. This sugar is used for dusting cookies and cakes.

Since the flavor of the vanilla bean is very strong, it lasts for a long time if preserved in an airtight jar. Each time you use some of the sugar for dusting cakes, refill the vanilla jar.

Basic Continental Spongecake

Continental cakes are never monumental in their appearance. At first glance they seem rather flat in comparison with certain cake-mix cakes. But the secret of Viennese-Hungarian cakes is that one should barely taste the basic cake or the pastry—the filling is what counts! You will find several recipes for filled spongecake in this chapter.

6 eggs, separated
6 tablespoons sugar
1 teaspoon finely grated
    lemon rind
1-inch stick of vanilla
    bean

¼ teaspoon baking powder
    (optional)
10 tablespoons cake flour
Butter for greasing tin

Beat the egg yolks with the sugar until the mixture becomes a pale lemon color. Add the grated lemon rind and the vanilla bean, split open and scraped. Add baking powder. Beat the egg whites until stiff. Fold into yolk mixture carefully, alternating with spoonfuls of sifted flour, and take care not to bruise the mixture.

Well butter a deep 8-inch cake pan or spring-form pan and dust with flour. Preheat your oven and bake cake in a 350° oven for 35 minutes.
(*Serves 8.*)

Easy Dobos Cake

(DOBOSTORTA)

Hungary

The real Hungarian *dobos* cake contains as many as eight wafer-thin layers of butter-spongecake. Each wafer is baked separately. The name *dobos* comes from the Hungarian word *drum* is given to this cake because of the hard caramel-sugar which is poured over the top, which suggests the drum from a military band. For the easy *dobos* cake, use your BASIC CON-TINENTAL SPONGECAKE, prepared a few days ahead and cut, just before you fill it, into as as many thin layers as possible without crumbling the cake.

BASIC CONTINENTAL SPONGECAKE, *cut into at least 4 layers*

The Filling:

    8 *tablespoons sugar*
    6 *egg yolks*
    ½ *pound dark confectioner's*
       chocolate, shredded
    ½ *pound butter*

For the Caramel Coating on Top:

    ½ *pound confectioner's*
       sugar
    4 *tablespoons water*

Put the sugar and the egg yolks in the top of a double boiler. Beat over the fire until a stiff custard is obtained. Off the fire mix in the shredded confectioner's chocolate and when cool add the separately creamed butter. Spread this cream over each sponge layer, but leave top uncoated. Coat also the sides of the cake with this chocolate cream.

To make the drum, put the confectioner's sugar with the water in a saucepan. Caramelize until golden in color. Immediately dip a flat knife into boiling water, pour the caramel-glaze on top of the cake and spread evenly with the wet knife. (*Serves 8.*)

Beethoven Cake

(BEETHOVENTORTE)

Austria

1 BASIC CONTINENTAL
  SPONGECAKE
4 tablespoons strong black
  coffee
3 egg yolks

9 tablespoons confectioner's
  sugar
½ pound butter
3 tablespoons roasted and
  chopped hazelnuts

Bake your spongecake at least a day before. Cut it into three layers. Fill each layer with the following cream and also coat the outside with it.

Prepare a very strong, espresso-type coffee. Cream egg yolks and mix with sugar. Put into a double boiler, adding the coffee. Cook while beating until a thick coffee custard is obtained. When cool, mix with the separately creamed butter. Sprinkle outside of the cake with coarsely chopped, roasted hazelnuts. (*Serves 8.*)

Giant Rum Cake

(ORIASI PUNCSTORTA)

Hungary

1 BASIC CONTINENTAL SPONGECAKE	½ cup orange marmalade
1 BASIC CHOCOLATE CAKE	Pink icing (sugar icing colored with a few drops of red food coloring)
6 tablespoons sugar	
¼ cup rum	
1 orange	

Prepare the 2 basic cakes at least 2 days ahead. Cut the sponge-cake into half horizontally. Cut the chocolate cake into small, inch-square cubes.

In a saucepan heat the sugar with the rum until melted. Remove from flame, add the juice and the grated peel of an orange. Soak the chocolate cake cut into cubes in this liquid for 2 hours.

Spread half of the spongecake with orange marmalade. Cover with the rum-soaked chocolate cake. Press down hard and place the second half of the spongecake on top. Cover with a large plate and put weights on top. Place in the refrigerator overnight. Coat the cake with pink icing.

(Serves 10–12.)

Basic Chocolate Cake

I use this basic cake whenever a recipe calls for a chocolate sponge. The cake can be filled with various creams and fillings, as you will see farther on in this chapter.

6 tablespoons butter	½ teaspoon baking
6 tablespoons sugar	powder
6 eggs, separated	8 tablespoons cake flour
5 ounces bitter	
confectioner's	
chocolate, grated	

Cream the butter and sugar with an electric beater (or by hand—it takes 20 minutes that way!). Add the egg yolks one by one. Fold in the grated chocolate and a pinch of baking powder. Beat the egg whites until very stiff. Fold them in the mixture, using alternate spoonfuls of sifted flour and egg whites.

Well butter and flour an 8-inch cake pan. Preheat oven to 400°. Put in cake, reduce heat first to 350° then after 20 minutes to 300°. Baking time is between 45 minutes to 1 hour, depending on your oven.

(Serves 8.)

Chestnut Cream Cake

(KASTANIEN TORTE)

Austria

1 8-inch BASIC CHOCOLATE CAKE *cut into 3 layers*

The Filling:

1 1-pound can chestnut
   purée (crème de
   marrons)
4 tablespoons sugar
2 teaspoons rum
Scrapings of a small piece
   of vanilla bean

2 cups stiffly whipped
   cream
Glazed chestnuts (marrons
   glacés) to decorate

Prepare your basic chocolate cake (preferably one day ahead) and cut into 3 layers. Fill between layers and coat the outside with the following cream:

In a mixing bowl put in the canned, unsweetened chestnut purée. Mix in the sugar, rum and the scrapings of a small piece of vanilla bean (or a few drops of vanilla essence).

Whip the cream and mix with the prepared chestnut purée. Spread thickly between layers and coat cake all over. Decorate with glazed chestnuts (and sugared violets, if available). (*Serves 8.*)

Raspberry Cake

(HIMBEERENTORTE)

Austria

1 BASIC CHOCOLATE CAKE *cut into* 2 *layers*

For the Filling:

1 cup fresh (or frozen)   1 cup ground almonds
    raspberries, crushed   Vanilla flavoring
1½ cups whipped cream

Bake your chocolate cake and cut into half horizontally. Use fresh or frozen raspberries (the frozen ones give an excellent result). Crush them into a pulp. If fresh raspberries are used, add 2 or 3 tablespoons of powdered sugar to sweeten. Frozen raspberries are already sweet.

Whip the cream until stiff. Add vanilla flavoring. Spread half the cream on top of the first layer of cake. Dust liberally with ground almonds. Arrange half the crushed raspberries over it. Cover with second half of the chocolate cake.

Mix the remaining cream with the crushed raspberries and use it to coat cake all over. Sprinkle with the ground almonds. (*Serves 8.*)

Black Forest Cherry Cake

(SCHWARZWALDER KIRSCHTORTE)

Black Forest

Cherries from the Black Forest are famous all over Europe and so is the *Schwarzwalder Kirschtorte*—a light chocolate spongecake filled with sour cherries and whipped cream. No book on the Blue Danube would be complete without this specialty.

4 eggs, separated	1½ cups pitted black
9 level tablespoons sugar	cherries
6 tablespoons water	2 tablespoons rum
¼ pound butter	½ pint cream, whipped
16 tablespoons cake flour	2–4 ounces dark
1 teaspoon baking powder	confectioner's chocolate
4 tablespoons cocoa	

In a mixing bowl put the 4 egg yolks, the sugar, and the water and beat (by hand 20 minutes or with an electric beater for 4 minutes). Soften the butter and mix in. Stiffly beat the egg whites and fold in, alternating with the flour, which was mixed with the baking powder and the cocoa.

Preheat your oven to 300°. Well butter and flour a 10-inch cake pan. Pour in the mixture and bake for 45 minutes. When cool, cut cake into 3 layers. (It is best to bake cake a day ahead.)

Pit the cherries, sprinkle with a little sugar, and flavor with

rum. Let stand for 1 hour. Stiffly whip the cream and sweeten to taste.

Arrange half of the well-drained cherries on top of the first layer of the cake and cover with one-third of the whipped cream. Cover with the second layer of cake, then cherries, again cream. Place the third layer on top and coat cake with the remaining cream. Very coarsely grate the dark confectioner's chocolate and sprinkle the outside of the cake with the chocolate shavings. Chill cake before serving.

(*Serves 8–10.*)

Orange Biscuit Cake

(NARANCSTORTA)

Hungary

This is one of my favorite stand-bys: a cake that needs no baking. It should be prepared the day before and, to facilitate unmolding, use a spring-form cake pan.

The Filling:

7 *tablespoons sugar*	3 *dozen ladyfingers or*
4 *egg yolks*	*sponge biscuits*
A little vanilla	½ *cup rum*
2 *large oranges*	½ *cup milk*
½ *pint heavy cream,*	*Candied orange slices to*
stiffly whipped	*decorate*

Prepare an orange custard by placing sugar in the top of a double boiler. Beat in the egg yolks one by one, add vanilla and the juice of the oranges. Add also the grated peel of 1 orange. Beat until custard thickens, then remove, and when cool mix in the whipped cream. Retain a portion of this cream for coating the outside of the cake, which is to be done the following day. Dip each ladyfinger or sponge biscuit into the rum-flavored milk and line the bottom and sides of your 8-inch spring-form cake pan. Spread with the orange-custard cream. Next comes again a layer of rum-flavored ladyfingers, then orange cream, then another layer of ladyfingers. Top layer must always be ladyfingers.

Cover and place cake overnight in refrigerator. Just before serving, unmold and coat the outside with the remaining orange-cream. Decorate with candied orange slices. (*Serves 8.*)

Lazy Cake

(LUSTA TORTA)

Hungary

½ pound sweet butter
4 tablespoons sugar
4 egg yolks
12 tablespoons
  ground almonds
½ cup rum

½ cup milk
3 dozen ladyfingers or
  sponge biscuits
Whipped cream to coat
  cake

Using an electric beater, prepare the filling by creaming the butter, sugar, and egg yolks. When smooth, blend in the almond meal. Take a 10-inch spring-form cake pan. Mix rum with milk and lightly dip each ladyfinger or sponge biscuit into this as you line the bottom and sides of the tin.

Spread generously with almond cream, then make a second layer of rum-flavored ladyfingers. Again cream, then ladyfingers. Continue using up all ingredients, taking care that the top layer is ladyfingers. Cover and place cake in refrigerator overnight. Just before serving unmold, coat all over with stiffly beaten (and lightly sweetened) whipped cream. (Serves 8.)

Walnut Cake with Coffee Cream

(NUSSTORTE)

Austria

The Cake:

1½ cups ground walnuts	5 egg whites
2 whole eggs	Butter and flour to
5 egg yolks	grease pan
2 cups sugar	
2 tablespoons sifted	
breadcrumbs	

Cream until smooth the walnuts with the 2 whole eggs, the yolks of 5 eggs, and sugar. Fold in the breadcrumbs, together with the separately stiffly beaten 5 egg whites. Butter well and flour a 9-inch spring-form cake pan. Preheat oven to 350°. Pour in mixture and bake ¾ hour. When cool, cut into halves, fill, and coat with the cream.

The Cream:

½ pound sweet butter
1 cup sugar
3½ tablespoons strong black coffee
1½ cups ground walnuts

Cream butter with sugar, add coffee and ground nuts, and beat until smooth.
(*Serves* 8.)

Daisy's Chocolate Cake

(SCHOKOLADE TORTE)

Austria

¼ pound dark confectioner's semisweet chocolate

2 tablespoons strong black coffee

¼ pound butter

½ cup sugar

8 eggs, separated

Butter and flour for greasing pan

In a double boiler soften the chocolate in black coffee. Beat butter and sugar in electric beater. When cool, add chocolate and, one by one, the egg yolks. Beat until smooth. Lastly fold into mixture, by hand, the separately beaten egg whites. Butter well and flour an 8-inch ovenproof dish which can go to the table. Pour in half of mixture. Preheat oven to 350° and bake 45 minutes. Cool. Spread second half of mixture over top and place in refrigerator to chill for a few hours. Slice in cake wedges. (Serves 8.)

Linzer Cake

(LINZERTORTE)

Austria

10 ounces butter	1⅔ cups sugar
3 cups flour	1 teaspoon cinnamon
1 whole egg	2 cups raspberry jam to
1 egg yolk	spread over cake
2½ cups ground walnuts	

Work the butter and flour together as if for short paste. Add eggs, ground walnuts, sugar, and cinnamon. Halve the mixture. Use a large 11-inch pie dish 2 inches deep and line with half the rolled-out pastry.

Preheat oven to 375° and bake for half an hour. Take out, spread with raspberry jam. With second half of pastry, cover in crisscross open latticework fashion. Replace in oven and bake at same heat another 30 minutes. While still warm, dust with VANILLA-FLAVORED POWDERED SUGAR.

(Serves 10.)

Sacher Cake
(SACHERTORTE)

Austria

It is rare to find an Austrian or Hungarian housewife who does not claim that her Sacher cake is the original recipe given to her ancestors by Frau Sacher, the gracious, plump, and efficient proprietress of the famous Hotel Sacher in Vienna. It is said that the original recipe is still in a strongbox at the hotel. My recipe is from my grandmother. The cake is best when baked twenty-four hours ahead.

6 ounces butter
6 tablespoons sugar
5 egg yolks
6 ounces dark
confectioner's chocolate,
grated
12 tablespoons flour

6 egg whites
Raspberry or apricot
jam to spread on top
CHOCOLATE GLAZE
Whipped cream served
separately

Cream butter and sugar with an electric beater. Add the egg yolks one by one and mix well. Add the grated chocolate and beat till the mixture is smooth. Separately beat the egg whites until stiff and fold them in, alternating with spoonfuls of sifted flour. Take care not to bruise mixture. Line an 8-inch cake tin with greaseproof paper. Well butter and dust with flour. Preheat your oven to 350°. Put in cake and bake for exactly 1 hour.

When cool, spread top with raspberry or apricot jam, coat with chocolate glaze.

The whipped cream is always served separately with this cake. (*Serves 8.*)

Basic Continental Chocolate Glaze

This glaze, which is different from chocolate icing, is used for Continental cakes, especially for the SACHER CAKE and the small ISCHLER COOKIES.

> 8 *ounces sugar cubes*
> 1 *measuring cup water*
> 8 *ounces dark confectioner's chocolate*
> 2 *tablespoons butter*

Put lump sugar in a saucepan and add the water. Boil, stirring all the time, until a thick syrup is obtained. Remove from flame, add the grated chocolate, beat until smooth and well mixed. When slightly cool, add the butter and mix well.

While the glaze is still soft and running, use it for immediate coating of the cake. To obtain a shiny glaze, dip a flat spatula in cold water and spread the glaze.

Never let this glaze set in the refrigerator, only in a cool place.

DESERTS

The Gugelhupf

Austria

Everybody who has been to Austria (or frequents an Austrian or Hungarian cake shop abroad) knows the *Gugelhupf*. This is a delicious coffeecake, baked in a *Gugel* mold, and liberally dusted with VANILLA-FLAVORED POWDERED SUGAR.

5 tablespoons flour	½ cup blanched, finely
8 tablespoons cake (or	sliced almonds
self-rising) flour	½ cup sultana raisins
½ pound butter	Butter and finely sifted
1 cup milk	breadcrumbs to coat the
5 eggs	Gugelhupf form
3 tablespoons sugar	VANILLA-FLAVORED
Juice and grated rind of	POWDERED SUGAR
1 lemon	to dust all over

In an electric mixer mix the flours and the butter, adding the milk and eggs one by one. Add sugar, the lemon juice, and grated peel, work into a light, firm dough. Mix in the sliced and blanched almonds and the sultanas. Let this dough stand in a warm place, covered with a tea towel, for about 1 hour.

Take your *Gugelhupf* form and butter it very well. Dust it with breadcrumbs. Pour in the dough and place in a pre-heated 350° oven. After 5 minutes turn heat down to 250°, then after 5 minutes to 200°. Baking time is 45 minutes.

While still hot, dust with VANILLA-FLAVORED POWDERED SUGAR. (*Serves 6.*)

Chestnut Purée

(GESZTENYEPURE)

Hungary

2 pounds chestnuts	½ cup sugar
1½ cups milk	4 teaspoons strong rum
Small piece of vanilla	Sweetened whipped cream
bean	

Cook chestnuts in boiling water for half an hour. Carefully peel off the outer hard and the inner furry skin. Place the cleaned chestnuts in a saucepan with the milk and a piece (about 1 inch long) of vanilla bean split open in the middle. Bring carefully to a boil, reduce heat, and let chestnuts simmer for another half hour. Sweeten with the sugar and add the rum.

Strain these chestnuts through a coarse sieve. (In specialty hardware stores one may obtain a chestnut strainer.) The purée should resemble thin spaghetti or vermicelli. It should be garnished with plenty of sweetened whipped cream and served very cold.
(Serves 6.)

Basic Unsweetened Puff Paste

1 pound butter	Pinch of salt
4 cups flour	1½ cups cold water

Put the butter in a tea towel and with a rolling pin beat to obtain an oblong slab. Keep this butter in the refrigerator until the moment it is to be used. Now prepare a very firm dough with the plain flour, salt, and cold water. Knead hard and roll out to a square shape. Take the butter out of the tea towel and let stand in a cool place for 20 minutes.

Roll out again, this time with the butter in the middle, and fold in 3. Roll again, this time in the opposite direction, and again fold in 3 and let stand for another 20 minutes. Do this procedure twice more, each time at 20-minute intervals. The more you fold, rest, and roll out, the flakier your pastry becomes.

Keep in a cool place until it is used.
(*Makes 2-crust pie.*)

Basic Short Pastry

1 cup butter or margarine	Pinch of salt
2½ cups flour	2 tablespoons sour cream
2 egg yolks	3 tablespoons water
1 tablespoon lemon juice	(lukewarm)

(*For sweet pies, tarts, etc., add 2 tablespoons of sugar to the basic mixture.*)

Cut butter into very small pieces. Put flour on a slab and work in the butter pieces with the tips of your fingers. Add the egg yolks, lemon juice, salt, sour cream, and water. Knead and work into a smooth pastry. Let pastry rest in the refrigerator for half an hour before rolling it out.
(*Makes 1 large pie or 2 small ones.*)

Christmas Walnut Roll

(NUSSBEUGELN)

Austria

This is the classical Christmas pastry, known in Austria as *Nussbeugeln*, in Hungary and Czechoslovakia as *Disobeigli*. It is prepared usually the week preceding Christmas, and the longer it keeps the better it is. There are two kinds of this loaf: one filled with walnuts, the other with poppy seeds.

To Make 2 Loaves:

1½ recipes of BASIC SHORT PASTRY

The Filling:

¾ pound ground walnuts
    (or 2 cups ground
    poppy seeds or
    poppy-seed roll)
Small piece of vanilla
    bean
1 cup milk
1 cup sugar
½ cup sultana raisins
½ cup finely chopped
    candied orange peel

4 tablespoons apricot jam
Juice of 1 lemon
Grated rind of 1 lemon
2 egg whites
Beaten egg yolk for
    brushing pastry
VANILLA-FLAVORED
    POWDERED SUGAR for
    dusting

Divide short paste in 2 parts. Roll each out in rectangular shape to a quarter-inch thickness. (The thinner the dough, the better the walnut roll.)

Prepare filling by putting in a saucepan the ground walnuts,

vanilla bean, milk, and sugar. Let simmer very, very slowly
for 15 minutes. Remove from flame, mix in the sultanas,
chopped candied orange peel, apricot jam, and the lemon juice
and grated rind. Separately beat egg whites and fold into the
mixture. Spread the pastry all over with this filling, then roll
up tightly and tuck in both edges. Brush with a little beaten
egg yolk, prick all over with a fork. Preheat oven to 350°. Put
in the loaves, but not too near each other, since they swell to
twice their size during baking. (Also, do not be upset if pastry
splits—the richer and better the filling, the more likely for this
to happen!) Bake 45 minutes to 1 hour.

While still hot, dust all over with VANILLA-FLAVORED
POWDERED SUGAR.

(Serves 10.)

Cottage Cheese Pie

(TUROSLEPENY)

Hungary

1½ pounds BASIC
    SHORT PASTRY
	Juice and grated rind of
	    1 lemon

1 pound cottage cheese	5 eggs, separated
6 tablespoons sugar	VANILLA-FLAVORED

Small piece of vanilla
    bean
	POWDERED SUGAR for
	    dusting

1 cup sultana raisins	

Divide short pastry in two and roll each loaf out in rectangular
shape—one to line the pan, the other to cover. The pastry
should be about a quarter inch thick and the tin long and
rectangular. Prepare the filling as follows: With an electric
beater beat the cottage cheese and sugar. Add vanilla bean,

sultanas, juice and grated peel of a lemon, and the yolks of 5 eggs. Beat until you obtain a smooth, creamy mixture. Fold in separately beaten egg whites. Fill shell with this mixture and cover over with the second half of the pastry.

Bake in a preheated 350° oven very slowly for 45 minutes. While still warm, dust top with VANILLA-FLAVORED POWDERED SUGAR. Serve cold, cut in 2-inch squares. (*Serves 8.*)

Apple Pie

(ALMAS PITE)

Hungary

1 *pound* BASIC SHORT PASTRY	½ *cup apricot jam*
1 *pound tart cooking apples*	4 *tablespoons ground almonds*
7 *tablespoons sugar*	*Beaten egg yolk to brush pastry*
½ *cup water*	VANILLA-FLAVORED
Juice and grated rind of 1 lemon	POWDERED SUGAR *to dust over*

Take a deep pie pan 8 inches in diameter and 4 inches deep. Divide short pastry in halves. Line bottom and side of the pan with thinly rolled out pastry and fill with the following mixture: In a saucepan put the peeled, cored, and finely sliced apples, sugar, water, and grated peel of a lemon. Cook very slowly until you obtain a smooth apple purée. Flavor with the juice of a lemon.

Spread apricot jam over the pastry lining and dust with the ground almonds. Fill with the cooked apples and cover top with the second half of the thinly rolled out pastry. Brush top with beaten egg yolk and bake in a 400° oven for 45 minutes. Dust with powdered sugar. Serve hot or cold. You may prepare this sweet in the same shape as your COTTAGE CHEESE PIE (see preceding recipe) and serve in squares. (*Serves 6.*)

Strawberry Tart

(ERDBEERENTORTE)

Austria

This is an open-face, meringue-topped tart that can be baked in a round or rectangular pan.

The Tart:

12 *tablespoons flour*	2 *egg yolks*
8 *tablespoons sugar*	8 *tablespoons blanched,*
⅓ *pound butter*	*ground almonds*

Make a short pastry with the flour, sugar, and butter cut up into small pieces. Add the egg yolks, the almonds, and knead well. Roll out thickly to the shape of your cake dish and press into the tin. Prebake for 35 minutes in a 350° oven.

The Filling:

2 *cups fresh or frozen*	*Juice of ½ lemon*
strawberries	3 *egg whites*
2 *tablespoons sugar*	

If you use fresh strawberries, wash them and cut them in half. Drain thoroughly the frozen strawberries first. The fresh strawberries should be sweetened with 2 tablespoons of sugar, but if you use frozen fruit, leave out sugar. Flavor only with the juice of half a lemon.

Heap strawberries thus prepared over your prebaked pastry slab (inside the tin). Have ready the stiffly beaten and very lightly sweetened egg whites. Spread this on top of the strawberries, return to a 300° oven, and leave there until the meringue is hardened.
(*Serves* 6.)

Salzburg Dumplings

(SALZBURGER NOCKERLN)

Austria

Salzburger Nockerln are one of the great specialities of the Austrian kitchen. They are creamy, feather-light egg dumplings with the texture of a soufflé. This is a simplified and easy recipe for an otherwise rather complicated dessert.

3 *eggs*	1 *tablespoon butter*
Small stick vanilla bean	VANILLA-FLAVORED
6 *tablespoons sugar*	POWDERED SUGAR
3 *tablespoons flour*	

Separate the yolks from the whites of egg. Take an inch-long stick of vanilla bean, split open, and scrape out the inside. Beat the whites of egg as if for a meringue, adding the sugar and the vanilla flavoring. Separately beat the yolks of egg, add 1 spoonful of the beaten egg white, and very carefully sift in some flour, alternating with spoonfuls of the stiffly beaten whites. The mixture must be fluffy.

Heat the butter in a frying pan, scoop out a big spoonful each time from the mixture and lightly fry on all sides, taking care that inside they remain creamy. (This is called the stiffening of the dumplings.) Transfer immediately to a warm plate and dust with plenty of powdered sugar. Serve at once. (*Serves* 2–4.)

Ischler Cookies

Austria

10 *tablespoons flour*	1 *egg yolk*
4 *tablespoons butter*	*Raspberry jam to spread*
3 *tablespoons sugar*	*between cookies*
3 *tablespoons ground*	BASIC CONTINENTAL
almonds	CHOCOLATE GLAZE

Put flour on a slab, cut butter into small pieces. Work butter well in with the flour, add the sugar, the finely ground, unbleached almonds, and the egg yolk. Prepare a crumbling short pastry with all these ingredients. Let stand in a cool place for half an hour, then roll out to biscuit thickness. With a cookie cutter one and a half inches in diameter (first dipped into flour) cut small disks from the pastry. Bake them in a 375° oven for 20 minutes or until very lightly golden.

When cool, spread raspberry jam over half the cookies and cover each with a second cookie. Coat with BASIC CONTINENTAL CHOCOLATE GLAZE.

(*Makes 18 Ischler cookies.*)

Vanilla Crescents

(VANILLEKIPFERL)

Austria

12 *tablespoons flour*	VANILLA-FLAVORED
3 *tablespoons butter*	POWDERED SUGAR *to*
2 *egg yolks*	*roll crescents in*
2 *tablespoons sugar*	
6 *tablespoons ground,*	
blanched almonds	

Put flour on a slab, add butter cut up into small pieces, and work in together till mixture resembles coarse breadcrumbs. Add the egg yolk, the sugar, and the almond meal, work to a smooth short pastry.

Shape pastry into a long sausage, cut off half-inch-thick pieces. Well flour your hands and, rolling a piece of pastry against a wooden board (or marble slab) shape first a long, thin sausage from it. Cut up sausage into 2-inch-long pieces, twist each piece to the shape of a crescent.

Place crescents on a baking sheet and bake in a 350° oven till dry and crisp. While still hot, roll each crescent in powdered sugar. These crescents can be kept for a long time in tightly closed cookie jars.

(*Makes 2 dozen small crescents.*)

STRUDEL AND ITS FILLINGS

I find it impossible to teach from a book anyone who has never seen strudel made. The basic strudel dough is very simple—only flour and water. But it needs to be a special flour and the consistency of the dough so elastic that 1 pound of it can cover the surface of a kitchen table. The strudel should stretch and stretch without tearing, and after the filling is scattered over it, you must roll it up tightly with the aid of a linen cloth.

Should you wish to try, here is the recipe for the dough:

Strudel Dough:

6 cups flour
  (preferably strudel flour,
  obtained from specialty
  shops)
2½ cups lukewarm water

Pinch of salt
1 tablespoon melted,
  lukewarm bacon fat
1 tablespoon vinegar

Mix all ingredients together on a wooden slab. Knead the dough hard (it is at first very sticky), beat with all your force against the wooden slab until dough is so well mixed and elastic that your hands are completely clean of all flour.

Divide into two, shape in round loaves, dust with flour on top, and keep in a warm place for 15 minutes.

Cover table with a coarse linen cloth. Sprinkle cloth with flour. Put dough in the center, and begin rolling it with a rolling pin. Now carefully stretch it toward yourself until the rectangular-shaped dough covers the entire surface of the table.

Let dry for 10 minutes, then brush surface with drops of

melted bacon fat. Spread with a filling and, taking the long side of the rectangular pastry, roll up tightly with the aid of the linen cloth. Repeat operation with second portion of pastry. Brush strudel with some more melted fat and bake in a 350° oven for 45 minutes.

(*Makes 2 large strudels or servings for 8.*)

Apple Strudel

(ALMASRETES)

Hungary

One recipe for STRUDEL DOUGH

Filling for One Strudel:

1½ pounds tart cooking
    apples
Melted bacon fat
2 tablespoons ground
    almonds

2 tablespoons finely sifted
    breadcrumbs
4 tablespoons sugar

Peel, core, and grate the apples. Brush surface of strudel dough with a little melted fat. Scatter with ground almonds and breadcrumbs, then over these the grated apple. Sprinkle with sugar, roll dough tightly, tuck in both ends. Brush top with more melted fat and bake in a 350° oven until crisp and golden.

(*Serves 4.*)

Fresh Cherry Strudel

(CSERESNYESRETES)

Hungary

Double recipe for STRUDEL DOUGH

Filling for Two Strudels:

Melted bacon fat	5 cups pitted, fresh
5 tablespoons ground	cherries
almonds	6 tablespoons sugar
2 tablespoons breadcrumbs	

Brush dough with melted fat, sprinkle with almonds and breadcrumbs mixed. Scatter liberally with cherries, sprinkle with sugar. Roll up, brush top with more melted fat, and bake in a 350° oven for 45 minutes.
(*Serves* 8.)

Cottage Cheese Strudel

(TUROSRETES)

Hungary

Double recipe for STRUDEL DOUGH

Filling for Two Strudels:

2 *pounds cottage cheese*	*Juice and grated rind of*
5 *tablespoons sugar*	½ *lemon*
3 *eggs, separated*	1 *cup sultana raisins*
Small piece of vanilla	*Melted bacon fat*
bean	

Cream the dry cottage cheese with the sugar. Add the egg yolks, a small piece of vanilla bean split open and scraped out, the lemon juice and grated peel, and the sultanas. Beat separately the whites of egg and fold in with the cheese mixture.

Brush your strudel dough with bacon fat, then spread over it the cheese mixture. Roll up and bake in a 350° oven for 45 minutes.

(*Serves* 8.)

Poppy-seed Strudel

(MAKOSRETES)

Hungary

Double recipe for STRUDEL DOUGH

Filling for Two Strudels:

½ cup milk
3 cups ground poppy
   seeds
8 tablespoons sugar

1 cup sultana raisins
½ cup apricot jam
Melted bacon fat to
   brush over

In a saucepan put milk, ground poppy seeds, and sugar. Bring to a boil, reduce heat, and let simmer for 20 minutes. Remove from flame, mix in the sultanas and the apricot jam. Let cool before spreading mixture over the strudel dough, which is first brushed with a little melted bacon fat. Roll up and bake in a 350° oven for 45 minutes.

(*Serves 8.*)

Savory Cabbage Strudel

(KAPOSZTASRETES)

Hungary

Double recipe for STRUDEL DOUGH

Filling for Two Strudels:

1½ pounds green cabbage, shredded	Freshly ground black pepper
3 tablespoons lard	6 tablespoons sour cream
Salt	

Shred cabbage finely. In a saucepan heat the lard, put in cabbage, season with salt and pepper. Cover with lid and steam, without any liquid added, for 45 minutes.

First brush strudel dough with a little melted fat, then dot with sour cream. Now spread out the filling all over the surface, season with some more freshly ground black pepper, and roll up tightly. Bake in a 350° oven for 45 minutes or until crisp and golden.

(*Serves* 8.)

Austrian Cream Strudel

(RAHMSTRUDEL)

Austria

5 slices white bread (or
    5 Austrian-type small
    rolls)
3 cups milk
6 tablespoons butter
7 eggs
Pinch of salt
Small stick of vanilla
    bean

Grated rind of ½ lemon
1 cup sour cream
12 tablespoons sugar
2 tablespoons fresh
    breadcrumbs
½ cup sultana raisins

Dip bread or bread rolls in milk to soften, drain and rub through a coarse wire sieve. To this pulp add the butter, cut up in small pieces, and work in well. Add one by one the yolks of 5 eggs, pinch of salt, vanilla, the lemon rind, sour cream, and 6 tablespoons of sugar. Beat mixture hard (or use an electric blender) and, when smooth, add the separately beaten 5 whites of egg, together with the breadcrumbs and the sultanas.

Shape into a long loaf, similar to a strudel, then twist this loaf in a way to form a circle. Put this in a deep, large baking dish. Mix the 2 whole eggs with the 3 cups milk, add 6 table-spoons of sugar and pour this over the strudel. Bake in a 300° oven for 45 minutes, basting it occasionally with the milk and egg-mixture until a golden crust is obtained.

Serve separately a vanilla or chocolate sauce with this dessert. (Serves 6–8.)

Basic Pancake Mixture for Desserts

2 cups flour	1 teaspoon cognac
2 eggs	1 teaspoon olive oil
Pinch of salt	2 cups milk

Put flour in a mixing bowl and break in eggs. Add salt, cognac, and olive oil and with a wooden spoon (or electric beater) mix ingredients well together.

Now slowly, while beating all the time, dilute with the milk until smooth and the consistency of running cream. Let stand before use for 1 hour.
(*Makes 8–10 6-inch crêpes.*)

Note: Never add sugar to your pancake batter even if pancakes are intended as a dessert. Sweeten it always with the filling, since sugar added to batter can often make pancakes stick to pan and difficult to turn.

Layered Pancakes

(RAKOTT PALACSINTA)

Hungary

10 *pancakes from* BASIC PANCAKE MIXTURE FOR DESSERTS

The Filling:

1 cup ground walnuts	½ cup sultana raisins
¾ cup sugar	3 tablespoons butter
Apricot jam	2 tablespoons sour cream
Raspberry jam	

Use your basic pancake recipe and prepare 10 pancakes. This may be done a day ahead.

Well butter a deep round cake dish (or ovenproof glass dish). Line bottom with a pancake. Spread with ground walnuts mixed with the sugar. Cover with a second pancake. This you spread with apricot jam. Next another pancake with walnut-sugar and a few sultanas scattered over it. Then pancake with raspberry jam. Continue alternating filling until all ingredients are used up. Top layer is pancake, which you dot with butter pieces and spread with sour cream. Put in a 300° oven and bake for 25 minutes.
(*Serves 6–8.*)

Walnut Pancakes

(DIOSPALACSINTA)

Hungary

8 *pancakes from* BASIC PANCAKE MIXTURE FOR DESSERTS

The Filling:

1 cup milk
1 cup sugar
1½ cups ground walnuts (or almonds)
3 tablespoons powdered sugar

Prepare basic pancakes. Have the filling ready, prepared as follows: In a saucepan put in milk, sugar, and walnuts (or almonds). Carefully bring to boil, then reduce and let cook, uncovered, until mixture is thick (about 10 minutes).

Fill each pancake with this mixture and roll up. Dust with powdered sugar and reheat for 5 minutes in the oven.
(*Serves 4.*)

Cottage Cheese Pancakes

(TOPFENPALATSCHINKEN)

Austria

8 pancakes from BASIC PANCAKE MIXTURE FOR DESSERTS

The Filling:

1 pound cottage (or cream) cheese	Vanilla flavoring
½ cup sugar	3 egg yolks
Juice and grated rind of ½ lemon	½ cup sultana raisins
	3 tablespoons sour cream

Prepare basic pancakes and fill with the following mixture: Cream the cheese with the sugar, add the lemon juice and grated rind, a little vanilla flavoring, egg yolks, and sultanas. Spread some of this filling over each pancake and roll up. Place on an ovenproof dish and spread sour cream on top. Brown under the broiler or in a hot oven.

These pancakes can also be made in layers, with cheese filling in between and crispened in oven.
(*Serves 4.*)

Cottage Cheese Spread

(LIPTAUER OR KOROZOTT)
Czechoslovakia-Hungary

It is difficult to pinpoint the country from which this well-known and much appreciated cheese spread originated. It is just as well known in restaurants in Austria as it is in Czechoslovakia and Hungary. However, since originally the cheese used for it was the Czechoslovak *Liptauer*—a sheep's cheese —in Austria the name of the dish became *Liptauer*. In Hungary one calls it *körözött*.

1 *pound cottage cheese* (or *sheep's cheese*)	2 *tablespoons chopped chives*
¼ *pound softened butter*	2–3 *teaspoons caraway seeds*
Salt	
Freshly ground black pepper	2 *anchovies, finely chopped*
1 *teaspoon Hungarian sweet red paprika*	3 *tablespoons beer*
1½ *teaspoons French mustard*	

In a mixing bowl cream the cottage cheese with the softened (but never melted!) butter. Add salt, pepper, and the paprika, continue creaming. Add the mustard, the chives, the caraway seeds, and the anchovies. Lastly add the beer.

Cream until a very smooth paste. You may use this as a party dip or serve as they do in Hungary, stuffed inside a hollowed-out fresh green pepper. Chill thoroughly and serve in thin slices. The green of the pepper makes a nice contrast with this pinkish cheese.

Baklava

(BAKLAVA)

Bulgaria

Baklava is a specialty of the Near and Middle East, a dessert of Turkish origin. It is served in slices 2 inches wide and 3 inches long and is very rich and sweet.

¾ cup ground walnuts　　　　½ cup melted cooking fat
2 cups sugar　　　　　　　1 cup water
1 pound BASIC
　UNSWEETENED PUFF
　PASTE

Mix the ground walnuts with a quarter cup of sugar. Divide puff paste into 3 portions, roll out each portion to knife-edge thinness in a rectangular shape. Place a layer of puff paste on a well-greased baking sheet, scatter all over with sugared walnuts. Cover with a second layer of paste, press down. Sprinkle with nuts. Continue till ingredients are all used up, with a top layer of paste. Cut up in slices. Pour over it the melted cooking fat, and bake in a 350° oven until crisp and golden brown, about 45 minutes.

Meanwhile in a saucepan cook a syrup with the water and the rest of the sugar. When the *baklava* is ready, immediately pour over it the boiling hot syrup. Let set and serve cold. (*Serves 6–8.*)

ENGLISH INDEX

FOREIGN INDEX